The Anointing of Ease

By V.K. Fields

2 The Anointing of Ease

The Anointing of Ease

by

V.K. Fields

Miracle Ministries Inc.
Raleigh, North Carolina

www.AnointingOfEase.com

The Anointing of Ease

ISBN 978-0-984-49671-6

Copyright © November 2016

Miracle Ministries Inc. – Raleigh, NC

Requests for permission:

Miracle Ministries Inc.

P.O. Box 18651

Raleigh, NC 27619

www.AnointingOfEase.com

Printed and published in the United States of America

Scripture references are King James Version (KJV) and New International Version (NIV).

The Anointing of Ease

Table of Contents

Introduction

Just like the weather, gravity, and the wind, the Anointing of Ease works on principle. You don't need to believe in weather in order for it to rain. You can outright reject the idea of gravity and still be drawn toward the ground and pulled toward the center of the Earth by gravitational power. Regardless of your acknowledgment or acceptance of the wind, it still blows and affects everything it touches—sometimes immediately and more often over extended periods of time.

Have you ever paid attention to the power of the wind? Whether a gentle breeze or a powerful gust, the wind is able to move and infuse motion into things that otherwise would be motionless or stagnant. Wind has the ability to bend and bow towering trees into submission. It blows lifeless tumbleweed for miles and miles across deserted plains and carves magnificent canyons out of stone and clay. Much like the wind, the anointing breathes life into dead or dying situations, revitalizing the life force of energy and translating it into movement.

If your life has become a difficult and joyless routine stuck in the status quo, then the Anointing of Ease may fuel the spiritual momentum you've been seeking. The Anointing of Ease is foolproof because it relies solely on the knowledge, words, and wisdom of your Creator; the Omniscient, Omnipotent, and Omnipresent One. The rules are simple because they aren't rules at all—they are promises. The only requirement is to activate your God-given Power, Authority, and Dominion (P.A.D.) as needed—utilizing the tools of Obedience, Faith, and Favor (O.F.F.).

Would you like for your life to be easier? It is simply a matter of your will, which should only be a reflection of His will. Everything you really need to know to have the life you really want is simple—and, more times than not, it's easy because you are a believer and a follower of Christ Jesus. Following Christ means that we study His life, follow His example, and generate results similar to His.

So, how do you do it? Without fail, every single day of your life must reflect an unwavering confidence and trust in God's Word and His ability to fulfill His promises to His children. There is absolutely no room for doubt or double-mindedness when it comes to complete and absolute trust that God has your best interest and outcome in mind. To walk and experience results of the Anointing is a recognition that there is a solution for every problem and that there is an answer for every situation you're facing that ultimately works for your good. Whether you like or agree with God's resolution to your problem is irrelevant and inconsequential; ease comes in the security of simply knowing that His way is better than yours.

Full enactment and implementation of the Anointing of Ease requires complete and total submission to the will and Word of God; an unfailing and unrelenting belief that God's plan and perfect will is always knowable, accessible, and obtainable in your life. In summary, here are some of the key points explained in this book for a life based on and built upon the Anointing of Ease.

Acceptance and Reality Check: It is what it is; but it will be what you make it.

Anxiety/Worry: No situation is bigger than God, so don't spend major time on minor issues. In other words, don't major in the minor.

Confidence: Don't doubt in the dark what you learned in the light.

Decision-Making: How you do anything is how you do everything. When there are no conflicts in your value system, making decisions is easy.

Emotional: Seek first to understand, then to be understood.

Financial: Earn more than you spend. Reject debt. Give more than you get—in order to get more than you give.

Forgiveness: Forgiveness is a gift you give yourself to escape being hurt repeatedly by the same situation.

Friendship: Listen more, talk less. To have friends, be a friend.

Grief/Loss: Earth has no sorrow that heaven cannot heal. We are temporarily here on assignment; ultimately, heaven is our home.

Happiness: No one owes you anything, and no one is responsible for your happiness but you.

Honesty: There are no versions of the truth.

Integrity: There is no right way to do the wrong thing.

Leadership: What you say isn't nearly as important as what you do. You are not leading if others are not following.

Love: Give and serve more than the other person; love is action. It is less important to be right than to be righteous.

Marriage: What can I give; and how can I serve? Every day I will choose to love.

Peace: This too shall pass. When it comes, let it go.

Perseverance: When life hits you hard, if you won't get over it, at least get on with it.

Physical: Eat less, move more, and cherish your body, which is a temple to God.

Priorities: The things that really matter are eternal and priceless; only what you do for Christ will last.

Problem-Solving: There's a point in the life of every problem where it's big enough to see, yet small enough to solve.

Protection: The favor of God surrounds you like a shield; no weapon formed against you will prosper. Always activate your faith force-field first.

Spiritual: Yes, Lord. Not my will, but thy will be done. Thank you, amen.

Stress: "No, thank you," is a complete sentence.

Success: What it takes to get something is what it takes to keep it.

Why?? Because He is God, and we are not!

1st Quarter ~ Take it Easy

Every single moment of every single day presents a new opportunity to make a different decision that can make things easier and positively alter the trajectory of your life for the better. It's really that simple.

Want something different? Do something different. Each one of us has the capacity to change our minds, which can and will ultimately change our lives. In your life, if you can change one thing, you can change anything; if you can change anything, you can change everything.

Contrary to how it seems, this beautiful existence on planet Earth was designed to be effortless and easy. As a result of sin, brokenness and the world's fallen state, it has become very difficult. In spite of those things, God's original plan for mankind still remains.

"Come unto me, all ye that labour and are heavy laden, and I will give you rest. Take my yoke upon you, and learn of me; for I am meek and lowly in heart: and ye shall find rest unto your souls. For my yoke is easy, and my burden is light" (Matthew 11:28-30, KJV).

Welcome to the Anointing of Ease

In the beginning God created the heaven and the earth. And God saw every thing that He had made, and, behold, it was very good. And on the seventh day God ended His work which He had made; and He rested on the seventh day from all His work which He had made. And God blessed the seventh day, and sanctified it; because He had rested from all his work which God created and made (paraphrase of Genesis 1 & 2).

In the beginning, God created a perfect world. In that perfect world, He placed people and gifted them with free will, which has choices... that can result in not-so-perfect consequences. A good man who makes a bad choice will encounter and endure the negative consequences of that choice.

God's original plan and intent for mankind was to live an unburdened life with an easy yoke. The redemptive sacrifice of Christ on the Cross once again has placed that divinely orchestrated and intended life of ease within reach for those who will reclaim it.

When it comes to the Anointing of Ease, to know it is to live it. And to live it is to love it. What good does it do to study God's Word, attend church regularly, fast and pray, tithe and give generously, and then live outside of

God's stated promises? If you are living a tormented, broken life of distress and unrest, then you are living beneath your God-given privilege and outside of His stated promises for provision. Once you internalize the peace and ease of God's original plan, never again will you tolerate the chaos, unrest, and "dis"-Ease that have been manufactured and dispatched to disrupt your life and to destroy your destiny.

God is not a paradox; in Him there is no contradiction. He is truth. He is love. He is just. He is real. If you believe that God is real, you must question why the Creator who loves us would want our lives to be hard, burdened, or unbearable. Love is an action, and the greatest level of love is service (love in action). God loves us.

The enemy wants your life to be difficult and filled with "dis"-Ease because he hates you. God wants you to have the gifts of peace, rest, and the gift of His anointing—and to experience the Anointing of Ease.

When it comes right down to the bottom line, all the things that really matter in life come easy. Salvation is as easy as A-B-C. **Accept** Jesus the Christ as Lord and Savior of your life. **Believe** that Jesus is the Son of God, who died for your sins, and rose again. **Confess** your sins, embrace forgiveness, and enjoy an abundant life that has been redeemed back to God. That's it.

If you take a look around, you'll see that most people are working very hard to earn or gain God's love, forgiveness, protection, blessings, and peace. However, the Word clearly states that those things have been freely given to His children. "Give, and it shall be given unto you; good measure, pressed down, and shaken together, and running over, shall men give into your bosom" (Luke 6:38, KJV).

"Peace I leave with you, my peace I give unto you: not as the world giveth, give I unto you. Let not your heart be troubled, neither let it be afraid" (John 14:27, KJV). "Judge not, and ye shall not be judged: condemn not, and ye shall not be condemned: forgive, and ye shall be forgiven" (Luke 6:37, KJV). "But the fruit of the Spirit is love, joy, peace, longsuffering, gentleness, goodness, faith, meekness, temperance: against such there is no law" (Galatians 5:22-23, KJV). And finally, "Stand fast therefore in the liberty wherewith Christ hath made us free, and be not entangled again with the yoke of bondage" (Galatians 5:1, KJV). What we learn from these passages is that many of us have opted for a life of "dis"-Ease because that's what we've been taught, and that is what we have seen and experienced all around us.

But the Bible teaches something different—that God has wonderful plans for us to enjoy the bountiful blessings of His creation. It is simply a choice of whether or not we will accept His gracious gifts.

The Anointing of Ease is not a mantra, vain repetition, or formula for receiving God's blessings. Rather, it is a system of behavior and belief, based on God's promises and His Word. Specifically, the Anointing is an ever-present spirit and a guiding life force that divinely inspires godly action. The concept of "Ease" refers to the amount of effort and energy required to experience the abundance of God's grace in our lives. It dispels the notion that life is a totality of suffering, sadness, and sacrifice. Yes, life presents instances of all those things—but not in isolation from God's healing presence, comfort, and guidance to lead us through and beyond the pain. The Anointing is what allows God's people to serve Him and enact His will on earth. In practice, the Anointing of Ease helps make it easier to live and serve God in an increasingly godless world.

Much like the wind, in the Bible, the Anointing is experienced as a rushing all-encompassing presence of the Holy Spirit. It cannot be seen, touched, or contained; only embraced and experienced. Scriptural references to the anointing describe an "unction" or compelling action. In the Bible, it was often symbolized by oil (anointing oil) to christen or appoint someone into an office; and it represented the presence of God's Spirit.

~ ~ ~ ~ ~ ~ ~

We must take great care not to confuse "ease" with laziness or slothfulness. In the parable of the rich man's barn, Jesus says, "And I will say to my soul, Soul, thou hast much goods laid up for many years; take thine ease, eat, drink, and be merry. But God said unto him, *Thou* fool, this night thy soul shall be required of thee: then whose shall those things be, which thou has provided? So *is* he that layeth up treasure for himself, and is not rich toward God" (Luke 12:19-21, KJV). The point is not to squander time and material riches with the intent of hoarding more, but rather to find comfort and encouragement in the rest, the peace, the blessings, and the promises of God.

To be clear, just because one walks in the Anointing, does not automatically mean that all of the challenges faced will require no sacrifice or pain; quite the contrary. What the Anointing provides is a sense of comfort and well-being; a sense of knowing that God's omnipresence and indwelling Spirit will be a light and a guide from beginning to end. The Anointing of Ease allows someone who is enduring a trying situation to focus on the outcome, not the process. Life cannot and should not simply be defined by one moment, because there are too many other moments that make it complete. In an online testimonial, a popular motivational speaker shared, "We are shaped by our trials, not defined by them."

First things first: The foundation on which we build upon for the Anointing of Ease is forgiveness. The acts of giving and receiving forgiveness create a clean slate for us to live and serve without hindrance according to God's will for our lives.

In Mark 11:24-26 (KJV), we find the following words: "Therefore I say unto you, what things soever you desire, when ye pray, believe that ye receive them, and ye shall have them. And when ye stand praying, forgive, if ye have ought against any: that your Father also which is in heaven may forgive you your trespasses. But if ye do not forgive, neither will your Father which is in heaven forgive your trespasses." So, why is it so important to forgive?

a. Forgiveness demonstrates our obedience to and love for God

b. Forgiveness releases us from carrying an unnecessary burden

c. Refusal to forgive provides an opening for your spiritual enemy and adversary to hinder blessings in your life

d. Forgiveness pleases God and opens the door for blessings

e. Serves as a powerful witness to others

f. Allows us to be forgiven

Easy Forgiveness Exercise

Who do I need to forgive? And, who will I release through my gift of forgiveness so that I too may be free?

1. _____

2. _____

3. _____

4. _____

5. _____

Prayer of Forgiveness: "Heavenly Father, I confess that I have harbored anger, bitterness, resentment, and unforgiveness in my heart toward the individuals listed above (say their names). Please forgive me for disobeying your requirement to demonstrate love and offer forgiveness. I repent and turn away from the sin of unforgiveness and ask you for the strength to release the hurt and offense that has occurred—and to freely forgive so that I too may receive forgiveness, release the past, and proceed with a clean slate. Thank you for loving me, and for forgiving me. I accept your forgiveness and thank you for your everlasting grace and mercy and the opportunity to begin again. In Jesus' name, amen."

Individual Reflection / Group Discussion Question:

○ **Why do so many people think it's OK to ask for God's forgiveness, and yet refuse to extend that same forgiveness to others?**

Notes:

_____

_____

_____

_____

_____

Book Club Discussion Prompts:

O In what ways do Christians excuse or overlook unforgiveness in everyday life, even though it is required by Scripture as part of God's plan and journey of salvation?

O Why do so many people struggle with unforgiveness/forgiveness?

O What are some of the consequences of refusing to forgive?

O Which areas of life tend to harbor the most struggle with unforgiveness and why?

O What techniques are helpful and effective in extending forgiveness, releasing the past, and moving forward?

Notes:

Planting the 'Seeds of Ease'

From this point forward, life as you know it can and will be easier. Repeat the following: "I will no longer accept the lies of this world that contradict the promises of God's Word for my life." Again. "I will no longer accept the lies of this world that contradict the promises of God's Word for my life."

It's time to put the Anointing of Ease into practice. To start, complete one task that will make your life easier, and then purposefully and prayerfully thank God for allowing you to do so. For example:

1) Pay off one small bill.
2) Send one overdue thank you note.
3) Politely, but firmly, say 'No' to one obligation that you cannot realistically commit to fulfilling.
4) Delete one aggravating social media account.
5) Apologize and seek forgiveness for one thing you know you've done wrong.

The point of this exercise is develop a habit of removing hindrances from your life that cause or foster dis-Ease. When you get in the habit of intentionally removing chaos from your life, you'll find that life gets easier and better.

Sometimes we are willing participants in our own unhappiness. If we're being truthful, some of the problems you're facing are your own creations. Some of the turmoil and unrest that you're experiencing… is your own fault. Let's just admit that sometimes we are the blame for whatever it is we're facing. And that's OK… God can still fix it, but we've got to own it.

When my nephew was in kindergarten, he was briefly the victim of bullying—some kid harassing and chasing him on the playground. He came home in tears and cried in my arms, telling me about the horrible day he had experienced. Here's how the conversation went:

"What's wrong?" I asked.

"This boy at school keeps chasing me on the playground," he said, trying to hold back his tears.

"Why is he chasing you?"

He shrugged his shoulders.

"Why are you running?"

He looked at me and shrugged his shoulders again, somewhat surprised by the question.

"What would happen if you didn't run?" I asked. "It seems to me that the only way he can chase you is if you choose to run away. When you go to school tomorrow, if he starts running toward you on the playground, I want you to stand still. He can't chase you if you don't run, OK?" He nodded his head and I gave him a big hug.

The next day, when I saw him after school, he practically jumped into my arms and said, "Aunt Val, guess what!! I was on the playground, and he tried to chase me, but I didn't run. And guess what?!... when I didn't run, he just walked away!" My nephew was so excited, and so was I. He found a solution to his problem, and I discovered a guiding principle that would serve me well for the rest of my life. Through that conversation with a 5-year-old, it became crystal clear that many times we are willing participants in some of our greatest challenges. All it takes is a refusal to take part and some problems simply will go away.

This commonly accepted notion that we are weak, helpless, defeated, and vulnerable targets in our world is a farce. It is a lie that the father of lies has told and that many unsuspecting saints have believed. Understand this: that in the army of Christ, you are always fighting from a Victory Vantage-point. Declare victory now, because the war has already been won. Your obligation is simply to stand strong against the adversary and not to concede any territory that has been secured.

Are any of these 10 Common Symptoms of Dis-Ease present in your life?: *(Check all that apply)*

□ Guilt   □ Anxiety
□ Shame   □ Disappointment
□ Worry   □ Fear
□ Stress   □ Disobedience
□ Doubt   □ Conflict

'Easy Does It' Exercise
In what ways have you participated in and encouraged your own unhappiness or dissatisfaction?

1. _____
2. _____
3. _____
4. _____
5. _____

Inspired by "The Anointing of Ease," and based on the responses above, what will you now do differently?

1. _____
2. _____
3. _____
4. _____
5. _____

Individual / Group Discussion Question:
What problems have I created that I also can solve?

1. _____

2. _____

3. _____

4. _____

5. _____

Notes:

_____

_____

_____

_____

Book Club Discussion Prompts:

O Is God obligated to come to your rescue when you operate in disobedience to His Word and will?

O How can believers know the will of God for their lives when there is no clear right or wrong answer to a problem?

○ Does God care whether or not His children are happy?

○ Is there a difference between joy and happiness; if so, what is the difference and how does it manifest in life?

Notes:

Human beings are notorious for making things harder than they are. As a rule, we over-think, over-analyze, and frequently misjudge situations because we are seeking some deeper and more profound meaning where one simply does not or may not exist.

Part of the practice in the Anointing of Ease is to minimize doubt and maximize faith. The desire is not to become blind to reason or logic, but rather to become open and accepting of God's Word on its face value. If we are told that 'Nothing is impossible,' then that's what it means—without caveat or equivocation. Consider this verse from 2 Corinthians 9:8: "And God is able to make all grace abound toward you; that ye, always having all sufficiency in all things, may abound to every good work" (KJV); or as it reads in the NIV version, "And God is able to bless you abundantly, so that in all things at all times, having all that you need, you will abound in every good work." That passage does not mean that God is able to bless you and extend grace unless it is related to bill collectors, the IRS, or student loans. It simply means what it means: all grace, all sufficiency, all the time. The question is whether or not you are where you're supposed to be, doing the good work that is required.

From Day 1 of the creation of mankind, we were equipped with the three-fold anointing of Power, Authority, and Dominion (P.A.D.). When you combine them, the result is a three-fold cord of strength that is not easily broken.

Any challenging situation that you face should be subjected to at least one component of this powerful arsenal. Sometimes you need to display strength through Power, force through Authority, and achieve Dominion through intercessory prayer. Reinforce those with Obedience to God's Word, Faith in His ability, and Favor (O.F.F.) to supersede the natural and to reveal the supernatural.

Life within the Anointing of Ease also will require a suspension of reality and an embrace of super-reality. That is accomplished by allowing the realm of divine supernatural influence to impact your day-to-day reality. In practical terms, you will live under the law of the land, with an understanding that the rules do not apply to you. Within what's legal and lawful, it is the perfect will of God—and only His will—that defines the heights of accomplishment for your life.

I don't gamble; however, I'm told the first rule of gambling is that the House always wins. Consider for a moment that whether we believe in God or not, we live in His House. We walk on His earth, breathe His air, and live by His established rules. Now, there's no denying that many people living in God's House are breaking His rules—but not without consequences. I want to encourage you to assert your authority as a child of God—living in His House—and benefit from the knowledge that His rules will always allow you to win. God's rules overrule any other authority in your life.

We are to be examples—living epistles—of what a victorious life should be. We are living, breathing testaments to the goodness of a kind, loving, generous, and gracious Father. We are earth-dwelling, law-abiding citizens of His Kingdom, serving as beacons of light and spiritual ambassadors to show others the way. We are called to be followers of Christ and leaders of mankind.

On a daily basis, we are to be spiritually clothed in the whole armor of God. Referencing Ephesians 6:11-17, those items include: loins covered in truth; a breastplate of righteousness; feet walking in peace; a shield of faith to block and subdue fiery attacks; the helmet of salvation; and the sword of the Spirit.

Notice that our entire wardrobe is made of defensive, protective gear. The only offensive "weapon," which we use to triumph in battle, is the sword of the Spirit, which is the living Word of God. In other words, when we are facing an adversary or challenger, we are instructed to speak the Word to secure victory. Since our starting place is from a Victory Vantage-point, we are always positioned to win: "Now thanks be unto God, which always causeth us to triumph in Christ, and maketh manifest the savour of his knowledge by us in every place," (2 Corinthians 2:14, KJV).

A couple of years ago, I was riding in the car with one of my nephews. He was young and broke, but wanted to take me for a ride in his car. It wasn't a brand-new car, but it was new to him. We got about a half-mile up the road and he said, "Aunt Val, my gas tank is on empty, can you help me put some gas in the car?" I said, "Sure."

We pulled into the gas station. I handed him my credit card and then started checking the email on my phone while I waited for him to get out and pump the gas. He leaned back in the window and asked, "How much can I get?" Without even looking up, I responded: "That's up to you." (Honestly, I was thinking to myself—'It doesn't matter to me how much gas you pump—get what you need, I already said it was up to you'). I don't remember how much gas cost per gallon at the time, but it didn't matter. He finished pumping the gas, got back in the car, said 'thank you,' and handed the receipt to me. I glanced at the fuel gage, smiled, and didn't say a word. He had pumped just enough gas to get the needle off of E-for-Empty. So, I don't know where he was going to take me to show off his car, but clearly, we weren't going far. I wondered to myself, 'Why would he only pump such a small amount of gas?' And then I had another thought: Wow, we do the same thing with God. We ask for something God already has said we can have, and then we don't have enough faith to receive what He's willing to give us.

We all know there was no amount of gas my nephew could have pumped into his car that would have mattered to me or affected me one way or the other. But he pumped gas according to his limitations—not mine.

My nephew is not the only person who has shortchanged his blessing. We approach God based on our limitations, and then we are disappointed when we don't have what we desire. When you falsely assume that your limitations are also God's limitations, then you short-circuit the possibilities for provision. God alone is your unlimited source, and everything else is a potential resource. There is simply no problem, situation, or circumstance that has God worried about whether or not He can handle it.

God's Word says that you can have everything He promised. Why not take it?

When things go wrong or don't work out, it's so easy to ask, 'Why me?' However, when things go right—just like we had hoped and prayed—how often do we wonder, 'Why me?' Almost never. As human beings, our default mode of understanding and appreciation is to anticipate that things should always go according to our will, but rarely to accept that sometimes our will is not in alignment with His perfect will. The lesson that we are to learn is that our obligation is 'To give thanks in all things,'—which is different than being thankful for all things. The latter is a forced response of insincerity, and the former is a mindset and expression of appreciation, gratitude, and confidence in God's divine order.

We know from Romans 8:28 that 'all things work together for good to them that love God and who are called according to His purpose.' That means sometimes things may not look good, they may not feel good, and they may not be good. However, in the ultimate plan for your life, all of those things (good, bad, or ugly) are working together **for your good.**

I grew up in a small Baptist church and served as an usher. There was a song that the choir used to sing titled, "Count Your Blessings." It went something like this: "Count your blessings. Name them one by one. Count your blessings; see what God has done. Count your blessings, name them one by one. Count your many blessings, see what God has done."

I don't know that I've ever literally counted my blessings. However, I've spent entire days just giving God thanks—from the time I woke up, until the time I went to bed. "Thank you for salvation. Thank you, Lord, for the ability to walk. Thank you, Lord, for the power of prayer. Thank you, God, for clean water to drink and to bathe in. Thank you, Father, for food in the refrigerator. Thank you for electricity and running water. Thank you for money to pay the electric and water bills. Thank you for the ability to make a living. Thank you for a beautiful home. Thank you for a nice car. Thank you for fresh air.

Thank you for the ability to walk outside. Thank you for the freedom to worship and praise you. Thank you for..." on and on throughout the day. Everywhere I went and everything I did allowed me to see new and familiar ways that God has continually blessed us. Yes, there is still sickness, disease, crime, and injustice in the world, but that's not new. Before there was evil, there was only good. And because there is good, evil will never win.

Easy Gratitude Exercise:
(Things I've forgotten to be thankful for)

SAMPLE:
1. Clean water
2. Genuine friends
3. Spiritual freedom
4. The right to vote
5. Education and literacy

My List of Things to be Thankful for:
1. _____
2. _____
3. _____
4. _____
5. _____

2nd Quarter ~ Easy Living

Be Free

Almost 20 years ago, I spoke at a Christian conference and retreat and opened with a Confession Session for the participants. This is a common exercise I use to break the ice and prepare the atmosphere for intercessory prayer. Essentially, I ask participants to clear their minds and hearts of any unforgiveness, which is a hindrance to prayer. As we went around the circle, each person sharing a tale of brokenness and unforgiveness, I was disheartened by the number of people who were still stuck in the same place and weighed down by hurts of the past. I was most concerned by the fact that so many Christians harbored so much unforgiveness, anger, even hatred toward others. In addition, many individuals had not forgiven themselves for past mistakes. They were still being haunted and punished by inner demons that played on their emotions and held them hostage in a guilt-laden, emotional prison.

It was so refreshing and liberating for us all to share in these words: 'God's forgiveness is free and it is immediate. Whom the Son sets free is free indeed, and from this moment on you will no longer define yourself by your past mistakes. God has given you an opportunity for a do-over, so take advantage of it and don't look back. Today, we are wiping the slate clean and beginning anew.' The same is true for you! Let's look at a few practices that can make your life easier.

What additional burdens are you carrying that can be released? Financial debt is a burden, and it's also a curse. Unforgiveness is a burden. Sin is a burden. Guilt and condemnation work in tandem to burden believers, who have been promised an assurance of rest in the arms of God. Confession is a very effective way to receive forgiveness and to unload a burden and head in a different direction.

Whenever I'm about to embark on a new project or head in a new direction, I tell myself to, 'Begin with the end in mind.' That means before I get started, I map out a plan for where I'm planning to end up.

'If you don't know where you're going, any road will take you there.' The end goal for believers is to fulfill God's divine purpose for your life and to live according to His will. Nothing else really matters, because only what you do for Christ will last.

Here's a daily practice that can make the process to achieving the Anointing of Ease even easier. Simply accept the premise that decision-making is easy when there are no conflicts in your value system. It might seem like the opposite is true, but it's actually easier to tell the truth 100 percent of the time than it is to tell the truth, say... 87 percent of the time, or 92 percent of the time. Why? Because once you commit to honesty and always telling the truth, it becomes your default habit.

For example—based on the statement above—how would someone determine which half-truths or untruths qualify for the remaining 13 percent or 8 percent? Do you mislead someone when it may avoid hurting their feelings—or when it's to your advantage? Will you lie only when it's more convenient and you have assurance that you won't get caught? How can you be sure you won't get caught? How do you know the lie won't backfire and require additional lies to cover the initial one? The energy and effort required to sustain the life of a lie is exponentially and consequentially greater than the amount of effort needed to simply tell the truth and deal with the resulting consequences.

I'm blessed with numerous opportunities to speak with and mentor young people. One of the things I frequently share with them is: "You need to know who you are and what you will or will not do before you have to prove it." In other words, the midst of a crisis or challenge is not the ideal time to define morals, values, and the principles that you stand for.

In small group settings, there's an exercise I do to demonstrate how easy it is to fall prey to temptation; and why we constantly need to guard our minds and hearts. I ask the students to raise their hands if there's someone in the group whom they do not know. Then, I ask a simple question: "Is it ever OK to randomly hit someone you don't know—and have no relationship with—for no good reason?" As expected, they all shake their self-righteous heads in unison, agreeing that they would never purposely "assault" someone they didn't know. The entire group agrees that such behavior is wrong. Until...

I then take out a $1 bill and ask a student volunteer whether they would be willing to "pop" another student whom they don't know on the side of the head. They confidently and quickly shake their head 'No' in refusal. OK...

I then take out a $5 bill and repeat the process. It only takes getting up to a $20 bill before the "hemming and hawing" of equivocation and justification kicks in: "Well, I don't have to hit them that hard, right?" Or, "What if I give them part of the money and we both benefit?" Or, "It's not like I'm running them over with a car; it's just a simple tap on the side of the head." Wow!

My next question to the group is: What happened?? Three minutes prior, 100 percent of the room said that this particular behavior was wrong, unacceptable, and unthinkable. Now, with $20 cash on the line, it's somewhat understandable and excusable—just like that. I cannot begin to tell you what people would be willing to do for a $100 bill. The lesson to my young students is twofold: 1) Don't be so quick to judge when other people make mistakes, because it can happen quickly, just as it did in the group exercise; and 2) If you'll do something you said was wrong for $20, under the right circumstances and with the right motivation, you'll do it for free.

Then I have them repeat after me: "My morals and values are not negotiable." *(Disclaimer: No students or participants are "popped" on the head or harmed during any group exercise).* The greater lesson is that once you define and commit to spiritual, personal, and professional boundaries, it's much easier to adhere to them when those limits are tested.

So, what's your price? Are your morals and values negotiable? What shortcuts are you willing to take if the price is right? Keep in mind that sometimes the price isn't monetary; rather, it's emotional or physical. By design, we are creatures of patterns and habits. How you do anything is how you do everything.

Are you frequently late to work? Then you're most likely late to church, late for a friend's birthday party, the family reunion, and any other event where you're supposed to arrive at a certain time. If you yell at your kids, you probably also yell when someone cuts you off in traffic, yell at your spouse, and use yelling as a way to express anger or displeasure. Is your car junky? Then your house probably is too, and your mind likely is filled with unnecessary clutter that keeps you preoccupied. Why?—**Because how you do anything is how you do everything.** People are creatures of habit. Once we develop a habit and build it into our daily routine, it takes more effort than it's worth to change or alter that habit, which eventually morphs into a pattern and becomes our default mode of operation.

If anyone is planning to change a habit, they first must change how they think about that habit. If there is a behavior that you don't like and want to change, the first step is to redefine how that behavior is viewed in your mind and in your life. For example, many parents consider raising their voices and yelling as a way to motivate their kids into action. If you want to stop that practice and discover an easier path, then accept the idea that yelling at your child (or children) is disrespectful to God and the precious gift He's given you in that child. Whether you're telling the child to put away their smartphone or clean up their room, when you're speaking to your child, remember, you're actually speaking to God's spirit in your child. What language and tone of voice would you use then? Your new demeanor de-escalates a challenging situation, models the behavior you want your child to emulate, removes the raw emotion, and also creates an atmosphere where you can thoughtfully and lovingly express your expectations and develop a new habit that makes the parenting path easier and more enjoyable. Just because your child is acting in a disobedient or unloving way, doesn't mean that as a parent you should fuel and validate that behavior. As their God-given guide and protector, any parents' job—without fail—is to set a standard of expectation for children to meet, by being a godly example.

You can't move backward and forward at the same time.
     If you are attempting to move backward and forward at the same time, it means that you are not moving at all. The resistance of holding on to the past, against the

pressure of trying to advance toward the future, essentially will immobilize you, resulting in no progress at all. Many people tend to get stuck in life because they are attempting to do both. To break that cycle, there are some things and possibly some people that you will have to let go. There are some wrongs that you will have to forgive. There are some hurts that you must allow both God and time to heal. In this spiritual journey, we all must come to the realization that every thing and everyone from our past are not suitable to accompany us into the future. To paraphrase Philippians 3:13-14, we must 'forget those things which are behind and reach forth to those things which are ahead, and press toward the mark for the prize of (or press toward the goal to win) the high calling of God in Christ Jesus.'

You can have it all, just not at the same time.

Superman does not really exist. Superwoman is a figment of someone else's imagination. Ignore the songs, comics, and movies. The idea that any human can or should repeatedly exert and exhibit "superhuman" strength to achieve unobtainable expectations for people they don't know is absolutely ridiculous.

Magazines and articles are filled with messages telling dads, moms, friends, spouses, employees, and bosses that they simply aren't good enough. Someone else is doing something—usually everything—better than they are. No one is ever good enough the way they are. We've all seen it: your belly isn't flat enough, your house is too small, your job is no good, your kids aren't talented enough to compete and succeed in the real world. But, you can have it all if you simply try harder; work more, and spend more to get the things you deserve.

Embrace the idea that you can have it all—if that's what you want—just probably not at the same time. As a matter of fact, why would anyone want it all at the same time? It seems like having a demanding career at the same time you have small children with whom you want to spend more time are in direct conflict with your greater life goals. Having the perfect beach body as a single 20-something is much more relevant than having it as a married 70-something retiree. A lot of money at 18 with very little knowledge or wisdom has ruined a lot of celebrity lives; versus having a lot of wisdom and compassion at 50—and the financial wherewithal to invest in making the world a better place. When we allow God's anointing to lead the way, we find that we can and will have exactly what we need when we need it—for His glory and not our own.

Years ago, one of our clients told me that she was a perfectionist; and then she proceeded to ask me if I was a perfectionist too. I answered very simply: "No, I am not." I explained that I do not strive for professional perfectionism, because it is unobtainable and unsustainable. We—referring to my team and I—strive for excellence, and excellence is our standard. Unlike perfection, excellence is a goal that we can always achieve.

God's mandate to us to be "perfect" means to be whole and complete in Christ Jesus—not free of flaws or imperfections. Perfection has already been accomplished in the life of Christ and His redemptive work on the cross, from which we can reap the rewards. A lot of people would be a lot happier and more at peace if they stopped attempting to achieve something that someone else wanted them to be.

The philosopher Aristotle said, "We are what we repeatedly do. So therefore, excellence is not an act, but a habit." The constant desire and pursuit of perfection in this natural life sets you up for failure. True success is rarely a straight line or problem-free process. True success often has errors and hard lessons, accompanied by thrilling triumphs and devastating disappointments. But most importantly, true success is the result of what you constantly and consistently do well, and that is making the pursuit of excellence a habit. We all have the potential and power to elevate ourselves and others through our spirit of excellence, our service to others, and our love for God.

Speak-Easy

Nothing should come out of your mouth that you do not want to materialize. Get in the habit of using words to shape the reality you want to live. Words have power. We know from Scripture that the power of life and death is in the tongue. Speak life. Speak peace. Speak ease. From the moment your feet touch the floor, the first words you utter should be words of thanks and gratitude. Everything after that should prophetically outline how the day will go.

"Every day is a good day, because every day is a God day. I'm excited that God is directing my path and using me and my life for His glory. I am blessed to be a blessing. I thank God that no weapon formed against me today will prosper. I have perfect peace through Christ Jesus, and all things are working for my good—even when it doesn't feel like it and I don't understand it. I will

not be deceived by what I see, because I know that God's messenger angels are protecting me and working behind the scenes on my behalf, according to His perfect will. The Creator of the Universe knows my name, and He has fully equipped me with everything I need to make it through today. When I don't know what to do, all I have to do is ask, because God freely gives the gift of wisdom to those who request it. Thank you, Jesus, for this amazing day!"

For the past decade, I've uttered the following prayer every single day—whenever I need a reminder of who I am and what I'm supposed to be doing: *"Father, anoint my steps and ordain my path."* Those simple words immediately realign my priorities and redirect my focus to the will of the Father. That straightforward petition also confirms that my desire is to be in God's perfect will and in a position to receive God's appointed blessings. In other words, when I am where I am supposed to be—doing what I'm supposed to be doing—the grace and mercy of God consistently meet me there and produce God's promised abundance and ease into my life.

From now on, you should expect good things to happen for you because God said that they will. It is important to understand: All the things that happen will not be good, but all the things that happen will work

together for your good—the greater good—to perfect God's perfect plan and His perfect will.

Speak-Easy Exercise

What words or phrases do you often use that may be undermining success and ease in your life? *(For example: "I am worried sick. I am scared to death. I don't know what I'm going to do. This is impossible.")*

1. _____
2. _____
3. _____
4. _____
5. _____

Individual Reflection / Group Discussion Question:

O **What areas of my life will be positively impacted when I change the way I speak about them?**

Notes:

_____
_____
_____
_____
_____

Book Club Discussion Prompts:

○ Using God's "Rhema" word from Creation as an example, what can believers speak into existence in their daily lives?

○ How can words build up or tear down the people who hear them?

○ "Sticks and stones can break your bones, but words can break your heart." Share an example of how this has played out in the media or in your own life.

○ How can the damage from hurtful or negative words be undone?

○ What and How can adults teach children to be mindful of their words and the power and influence that words have in their lives?

Notes:

Live Easy

Have you ever wondered why some people seem to be at total peace with their life and circumstances? They walk confidently through each day as though they don't have a care in the world. Why don't these people seem worried or stressed out? How do they always seem to be happy and carefree? What do they know that you don't know? They have embraced the Anointing of Ease.

Obviously, people have problems that need resolutions. But the Anointing of Ease conveys a sense of confidence and faith that whatever the outcome, 'It is well.' When we seek to determine an outcome and limit it based on our knowledge and expectations, we close the door to God's plan and also set ourselves up for disappointment. The Anointing of Ease takes priority over what you want and accepts what is the perfect will of God—without question and without fail. This particular anointing allows individuals to focus, pray, and give a situation everything they have—and still find joy and peace in the outcome, no matter what it is.

If you're wondering how to embrace and adopt a life of ease, then there are some basic principles and beliefs that you must accept:

a. God knows better than you; complete trust in Him is mandatory;

b. There is a God-ordained solution for every problem or situation you encounter;

c. God's will is the only acceptable resolution to your problem or petition.

Seek first to understand, then to be understood.

The Anointing of Ease gives people the benefit of the doubt—even if they don't deserve it; meaning, there's a reason why people act rudely, speaking sharply, or otherwise spread toxic negativity wherever they go. Doesn't make it right, but it's just easier to put some distance between you and other people's bad behavior—instead of allowing someone else to control your emotions or rob you of the happiness and joy you desire.

We simply don't know what someone else is experiencing at any given moment. That's why the Bible encourages us to use kind words in conflict. People everywhere are hurting, struggling, and battling with any number of issues; while believers are equipped with the joy of the Lord, God's promises, angelic protection, the Anointing of Ease, and much more. Honestly, it's just easier to be kind and loving, especially when others aren't deserving of our kindness and love. That's what God does for His children each and every day—He loves us despite what we deserve.

Think about this: The only times in the Bible when Jesus was angered was when He was dealing with the "church people." To the outcast of society, Jesus was kind, compassionate, forgiving, and understanding—because they were lost sinners seeking solutions. Did He overlook or excuse their sin? No, but He didn't belittle them or treat them as unsalvageable rejects. He loved them. He cared for them. And He instructed His people to do the same. Ironically, His perfect love exposed their sin and drew them into repentance.

Based on this truth and the presence of so many lost and hurting people in the world, why is it that the Church has a reputation for being mean-spirited, hateful, and judgmental? It is only by sincerely demonstrating the kindness, compassion, and love of Christ that we can make a difference in our nation and in this world. We must show love. We must show compassion. We must show kindness. We must invite people to come as they are and make room for God's Spirit to change their hearts and minds.

You may be asking: In our war-torn, reality-television world that elevates the depraved and ridicules humility and righteousness, how can we possibly feel encouraged? My response has consistently been that God's Word is 'a lamp unto my feet, and a light unto my path' (Psalms 119:105). Lights and lamps are only effective in darkness. When it's daytime and the sun is radiating above, we easily overlook or take for granted the benefit of light. It is when darkness descends and evil appears to prevail that the light becomes a source of comfort, guidance, and protection that beckons to the lost. Light shines in darkness.

~ HALFTIME ~
'ANOINTING OF EASE' LIFE COVENANT

I, _____ (insert your name), from this day forth, do commit and dedicate my life to Godly service, prayer, praise, and worship; and to only speak words of faith and demonstrate LOVE in obedience to the Word of God. This is my daily confession and acceptance of God's promises:

1. God loves me; and I will praise Him, for I am fearfully and wonderfully made in His image: marvelous are His works, and that my soul knows well (ref. Psalm 139:14).

2. I love, cherish, and respect myself, which allows me to offer the same to others (ref. Ephesians 5:3-5).

3. I will love, cherish, respect, and honor my body, because it is the temple of God and the dwelling place of the Holy Spirit (ref. 1 Corinthians 6:18-20).

4. I can love others only when I love myself; I will ask for forgiveness and grant forgiveness as a matter of spiritual principle (ref. Romans 13:8-10).

5. I will only speak positive words of life that align with the Word of God; I affirm that God has a glorious plan for my life, and I will not settle for less than His best (ref. 1 Corinthians 2:9).

6. I will only communicate with love and understanding, and I will demonstrate the love of Christ through my actions (ref. 2 Corinthians 13:11).

7. Because I love God, I can love others (ref. 1 John 4:21).

8. I will not allow the devil to deceive, confuse, or discourage me because he is a liar, and he hates the things of God. I have total victory in Jesus Christ (ref. Romans 8:1).

9. The power of life and death is in the tongue, and I will speak life to every situation I face and prophesy according to the perfect will and Word of God (ref. Proverbs 18:21).

10. For God so loved the world, that He gave His only begotten Son, that whosoever believeth in Him should not perish, but have everlasting life. God wants me to be saved and spend eternity in heaven with Him by accepting Jesus Christ as my Lord and Savior.

I willingly accept the anointing and life of ease that has been promised to me in Scripture (ref. John 3:16 and Matthew 11:28-30).

-----------------------------------   -----------------
   Your Signature   Date

3rd Quarter ~ Easy Does It

I'm often asked about how to apply the Anointing of Ease to legitimately hard situations or difficult life circumstances and difficult people. If you regularly watch the news or listen to politicians, it would be easy to think that all is lost and there is no hope for redemption. However, that is not the case. Even in the midst of chaos, there can be peace. Remember that the calm is found in the middle of the storm.

My life's calling of ministry requires countless encounters with disappointments, grief, sickness, sadness, mortality, and death. The perspective that heals the recurring heartache is that we must release the earthly to gain the heavenly. The purpose of this life is preparation for eternal life. All the more reason to spend life in loving ease as opposed to enduring a distressed life filled with dis-Ease.

Have you ever tried to help someone who didn't want to be helped? How often have you tried to be a one-man or one-woman rescue operation for someone who simply didn't want to do anything differently or better? Yes, you prayed and fasted; but you also made excuses for them, bailed them out of dicey situations, tolerated their poor behavior, rationalized their poor judgment, and took ownership and responsibility for their actions. How did you feel during that process? Did you feel better? Or did you feel exhausted, betrayed, and disappointed that even though you tried everything you could think of, they kept doing the same old thing?

We should all be in support of helping others and giving people a helping hand. But, I'm not a fan of trying to make grown people do anything. If the Father, Son, and Holy Spirit haven't changed them yet, we certainly cannot. For people who are an emotional drain on your life, it's time to give yourself a break and permission to love them from a distance. That means while we don't abandon people whom we love and who clearly need our support, it also means that we give them enough room to live, grow, and learn from their mistakes—and to accept the consequences of their choices. You are not responsible for other people's decisions or anyone else's happiness. Not your spouse. Not your adult children. Not your co-workers. Not your friends.

In ministry, I cannot even count the number of people I've met who have allowed other people to make their lives miserable. They have been emotionally drained and financially bankrupted while attempting to control another person's behavior. It simply doesn't work. Embracing the Anointing of Ease will release you from the burdens of guilt and condemnation and allow you to rest in the promises of God, who has given you complete assurance that your intercessory prayers for family and friends will be heard.

The truth is sometimes people act in ways that make them hard to love. But our job is to love them anyway. Friends, family, and perfect strangers all do things we don't like or agree with. How then are we supposed to live a life of ease when so many surrounding things and situations make us feel un-Easy? Matthew 13:30 talks about the co-existence of 'wheat and tares'—or grain and weeds—in God's harvest. Basically, we cannot fix, change, or force people to become something they do not want to become. Scripture instructs us to simply let the wheat and tares grow together, and He will manage the process of separation and judgment. We are to: Trust God and Love people.

1 Peter 4:8 tells us that love alone will cover a multitude of sins. Therefore, in our daily walk, we should simply demonstrate the love of Christ to all. When legendary activist and heavyweight boxing champion Muhammad Ali died in 2016, numerous television networks aired some of his most iconic images and quotes; one of my favorites is this: "If you love God, you can't love only some of His children."

Many situations seem out of reach and out of our control. We do everything we know to do and things just don't seem to work out the way we want. Let's consider a few of the most common areas, related to illness, grief, death, and loss (of life).

In a nutshell, there simply are no guarantees in life; certainty is only available in Him. Whether or not we plan for it or prepare for it, people whom we love and rely on may choose to be unkind and not love us back the way we desire. Children can get sick and parents can walk out, never to return. Spouses may betray our trust, and jobs may disappear without any warning. Every single one of those things happens every single day. Yet, we find a way to move on because time only moves forward.

One of the hardest truths of life is to accept that we all will die. Every single one of us. And there are just too many things in this world that you can die from to think that somehow we will escape them all. But why so early, you might ask? Why do babies get sick and die? Why do teenagers die? Why do healthy people die? Why do good people leave before we think they should? I don't know. And neither does anyone else. But they were always going to die—it just happened to be sooner rather than later. That's why it's so important to live our lives on purpose, in purpose and with purpose. On purpose. In purpose. And with purpose.

I understand that message provides little comfort when your heart is broken, but it should be great encouragement to know that there's more to life than what we're currently experiencing. There's more to the entirety of eternal life than the temporary negativity, jobs we hate, disappointment, stress, worry, frustration, depression, and constant threat of terrorist attacks. As believers, we should wake up every morning with a renewed sense of purpose that we have been called to accomplish something for God's glory that day. It might be a great feat or a small task, but it ultimately glorifies our Father in heaven, and that's really all that matters.

For the saints of God, it's important to remember that this world is not our home. Don't tether or mortgage your life to a world that's going to pass away. Live your life in a way that glorifies God and ensures that you have a home in heaven one day—where you'll again see those loved ones and be reunited with them forever.

Personally, my approach toward any of these challenging issues is the same as it is for anything else. Years ago, I changed my mind, which in turn changed my life. For me, I envision that my life is an assignment with a temporary job agency—and I'm here on earth simply fulfilling an obligation. Heaven is my "home office," if you will... and I've been dispatched here to accomplish specific tasks, goals, and objectives. I have a general idea of how long my assignment is supposed to last, but just like anything else, things change and jobs evolve. Regardless of what happens while I'm working here on my assignment, ultimately I will return to the home office and move on to the next phase of my spiritual career. If and when you choose to accept life as an assigned role that has no guarantees, then it's much easier to navigate the ups and downs and approach life in a more carefree manner.

Only when we are willing to release ownership of life and loved ones—and detach ourselves from material and temporal things—can we truly be free and experience the Anointing of Ease that God promised.

Un-Easy

I remember the first time I heard the word "malignant." Until 1992, it was not even a part of my vocabulary. I was in my dorm room at college, on the telephone with my mother. She told me that her doctors had found a tumor, and it was malignant. I didn't know what that word meant, but instantly, I knew exactly what that word meant.

From that phone call until the day she died, a total of six weeks passed by.

A couple of weeks after the initial call, I was visiting her again on the weekend. She had been moved from the hospital and was back at home—presumably to be in a familiar setting when she transitioned from this world to the next. During my three-hour drive home to see her, I spent most of the time praying about how to respond when I saw her deteriorating condition. I wanted to be brave, and I wanted to be strong. But, most of all, I wanted her to be physically healed. That wasn't going to be the case.

I walked into the room and in as cheerful and hopeful a voice that I could muster, I said, "Hi, Mommy!" She looked up at me through sunken, jaundiced eyes and said, "Well, who are you?" I was shocked to the point of devastation. I said, "Mommy, it's me, Valerie—your baby girl." She paused, stared at me and slowly said, "No, I don't believe I know you." I thought I would collapse onto the floor. To this day, that has been the most heart-breaking moment of my entire life. Tears welled up in my eyes, and the lump in my throat rendered me speechless.

I left her side for a couple of hours so that she could take a nap and so that I could gather my emotions and regroup. I spent most of the time praying and reminding myself that it was her illness and strong medication that had caused her to forget who I was... and nothing more. I prepared myself for the possibility that she might never remember me again. I gave myself a pep talk and mentally prepared for whatever she might say when I returned to her side.

When I walked back in the house and stood beside her bed, she immediately recognized me. She said, "There's my baby." After she spoke those words, I was inconsolable with tears of joy and overwhelmed with relief. I shared with her that she had not recognized me earlier. And her response was, "I could never forget my baby."

My mother knew she was going to die, and she was at peace. Because she loved me, she was honest with me and helped me to be at peace as well. We talked and she reassured me that my life would be everything I hoped for—even if she wasn't there with me in person to witness it. She let me know that she was OK and that I too was going to be OK. I will forever be grateful for that gift, because I know for a fact that level of peace only comes from God.

Even in my darkest moment, the Anointing of Ease was there to lift the burden of heaviness, relieve the weight of sadness, and eventually restore the joy I lost as I mourned. It has been decades since she passed, but I remember being thankful that everything I needed to tell my mother had been said. There was no regret and there were no unresolved issues. There was only love.

When you love someone and they fail to acknowledge the love you shared (intentionally or not), it is as though your entire history and relationship with them has been erased. The thought of my heavenly Father saying, 'Depart from me, I know you not' would be unbearable. The lesson I learned from my mother's bedside was to live a life that was pleasing to God so that He would never forget me, deny me, or disown me. The day my mother died was the day I made a commitment to live my life in such a way that I would one day see her again.

The reality for us now is that in our fallen world, people are going to die. There are no guarantees while we live; and if Jesus tarries, the only way out is death. People fear death when they idolize life, erroneously valuing a temporal earthly existence above a promised eternal redemption.

The seeds we lovingly sow in life should produce a bountiful harvest of saved souls for God's kingdom and guide us to the ultimate family reunion in which we will rejoice together forevermore.

The Best Prayer I Ever Prayed

"Lord, deliver me from the opinions of people."

That was the best prayer I EVER prayed—more than 20 years ago. When I was released and set free from the imagined judgment and condemnation of people whose opinions don't matter, my life was instantaneously changed and improved for the better. *Pray that same prayer, and your life will never be the same!*

How many of us agonize over what other people think; about what we wear, about what we say, about what we do, about how we look; about what we drive, who we marry, how we raise our children, how we decorate our homes, how much stuff we have, etc.? If you are making decisions based on the thoughts and opinions of people instead of the Word and voice of God and the leading of His spirit, you will regret it. Only what you do for Christ will last.

As a child of God, your ultimate accountability is vertical (to God), not horizontal (to people); so when God is pleased, you will certainly surpass the imposed "standards" of this world. Part of the danger in trying to live up to the expectations of others is that those expectations change—often and unexpectedly. One day you're supposed to be one thing; the next day you're supposed to be or do something different. Human feelings and emotions are fickle and unreliable at best. But we have an assurance in knowing that God's Word is unchanging and that the God we serve is the same yesterday, today, and forever; and His expectations of us remain constant. The best that people have to offer is a limited worldview based on their own life and experiences that may or may not be relevant to the path you're called to walk. We are clearly admonished in Scripture to 'trust not in the arms of flesh because ultimately, they will fail us.' Our obligation is to trust God and love people.

Consider a few examples of characters in the Bible who received a blessing or healing or experienced a manifestation of God's greatness by ignoring the popular opinion of the day. The well-known woman with the issue of blood had been given a negative diagnosis, a dire prognosis, and a dreary outlook for her life. It was unseemly that she should even consider the notion of approaching Jesus—the righteous teacher—the Master and leader of the disciples. How dare she even entertain the idea of invading His presence with her sick, filthy, and diseased body. But the woman pressed her way, against the opposing force of the crowd, and made her way to Jesus. Even though popular opinion and discerning looks from others would have told her to stay away and mind the customs of her culture, her spirit was drawn to the Spirit of God, which drew her closer to Him and His healing presence.

How about the woman who was caught in the very act of adultery? What stands out about this passage is how the ruling opinions of men were so condemning of this woman. The story clearly states that she was caught in the act—presumably not alone, right? But the opinions of men in that day dictated that the man was guiltless, while she was guilty. There is no mention of her partner being stoned to death for also being caught in the act of adultery. As the accusers prepared to punish her, Jesus stepped in and offered these words: "Let he who is without sin cast the first stone." Then they all dropped their stones and walked away. Jesus then asked, "Where are your accusers?" and she realized that she had none. When left to the judgment of people, we are all condemned and convicted. When justified by faith and covered by the blood of Jesus, we understand that God's grace is sufficient and that His mercy is from everlasting to everlasting.

Last, we learn from the Bible that the very opinionated Sadducees and Pharisees—so called experts and scholars—didn't want Jesus to heal on the Sabbath. They wanted to know why the disciples didn't follow certain hand-washing rituals. They wanted to know why Jesus would dare spend time with tax collectors and men/women of ill repute. In their opinions, these "other" people were unworthy. They didn't want children to approach Jesus. They did not want the woman with the alabaster box of ointment to come near him and anoint His feet because it looked inappropriate. They didn't want Jesus to go into certain people's houses to heal their servants because it might ruin His "brand" and reputation or send the wrong message. And what did their varying opinions accomplish? Nothing—except get in the way of and distract from the great work that Jesus was called to do. The beauty of each story is that Jesus was free from the opinions of people; so He healed them anyway; He delivered them anyway. He fed the hungry, blessed the multitudes, changed their lives and forgave their sins… in spite of popular opinion.

"Why Some Prayers Get Answered, and Others Don't"
Have you ever been disappointed because you prayed and prayed and prayed—but nothing happened? Or have you seen God answer someone else's prayers and seemingly ignore yours? Without question, this journey of salvation can often be confusing and challenging. However, the true test of faith is whether we will trust God completely—regardless of our circumstances—and even when He says "no" to us. I sincerely believe that one day we'll see the big picture and thank God for the prayers that He didn't answer the way we wanted Him to.

For those of you who cannot come to grips with the reasons behind unanswered prayer, allow me to share this perspective: God always answers prayer based on His Word, based on His Will and to His glory. The problem with that for us is that often we know the Word and we understand His will, but we don't always know His plan. The disconnect occurs because we have our own plans. The problem develops because our plans are within "time" and God's plans are throughout eternity.

Even when Jesus prayed, He did so humbly with godly submission, saying, "Not my will, but thy will be done." And honestly, if it's good enough for Jesus, it's going to have to be good enough for us. The reality is that we simply want what we want; when we want it. We want prosperity, abundance, healing and no problems, trials, or tribulations. Or, at least, that's what I want. Maybe it's just me, but I doubt that. And there's nothing wrong with wanting good things that bring God glory. However, we want them all within the span of 80, 90 or 100 years, which is barely a blink of the eye within the spectrum of eternity.

Over the years, I've altered how I think about things and how I pray about things. And the more I read, study, learn and grow, the shorter my own personal prayer list becomes. For the most part, material things have come off because I know now that they don't really matter, and they don't have any eternal consequences. I also stopped praying for other people to change or behave differently, because the moment you point out a problem with somebody else to God, He immediately starts working on you. Mahatma Gandhi's famous philosophy is clearly based on God's principles: You must be the change you want to see in the world. If you want things to change in your life, God changes you, and then you see and do things differently.

Several years ago, I conducted a prayer session on Answered Prayer. And I plainly said that God always answers. That's true. Sometimes the answer is yes. Sometimes the answer is no. And sometimes the answer is wait. So the question becomes what we should do when it seems the answers are consistently 'no.' Generally, that's a very good indication that it's time for us to review and consider our motives and motivation for asking. Are our prayers selfish? Are we asking for something because we don't want to be inconvenienced? As much as I hate to admit it, the hard time and trials of life are what strengthened me, and built my character, and gave me the ability to do the things that God created me to do. I would much rather have traveled the road of least resistance where the hardest thing I ever faced was whether to sing in the choir or serve on the usher board, but that's beneath the calling I have.

In ministry, I'm often required to aid and assist under the worst possible circumstances. Someone is sick, someone is dying. Someone is dead. Someone is falsely accused. Someone is in jail. Someone is homeless or starving. Someone is depressed and suicidal. It's always someone, and it's always something. So how, I ask you, would I ever be able to understand the disappointments these people feel if I'd never experienced my own? Sometimes unanswered prayer develops empathy for others. Sometimes it serves as a powerful demonstration of faith—the ability to simply trust God and have confidence in His Word even when it hurts and even when you don't understand.

For generations, it has been taught from platforms and pulpits that sadness and suffering are signs of piety, purity, and goodness; that the righteous should needlessly suffer for God's glory. Some religious doctrines also teach the concept of lifelong suffering as a pathway to perfection. However, the Bible teaches earthly suffering as temporary, purposeful, and minor in comparison to the promised eternal bliss of heaven.

How then is it possible to live an existence based on the Anointing of Ease while still experiencing suffering? That's similar to asking how anyone could possibly laugh if they've ever cried. In essence, a person cannot know, understand, or appreciate one without the other. There is no context for comprehending peace if there has never been chaos or confusion. There is no manifestation of ease without the discomfort of dis-Ease. The Anointing of Ease does not negate difficult life lessons, but it does allow believers to put those difficult situations into perspective and embrace hope for a blessed outcome.

When we are enduring a period of suffering, it is easy to feel isolated and alone—as though no one else has ever experienced loss, sorrow, disappointment, or failure. That's what your spiritual enemy wants you to believe and accept. But, it's simply not true. Everyone has experienced all of those feelings and emotions, albeit at different times and in different degrees.

People do not suffer in isolation. There are no new problems—only the same problems presented in new ways. The Bible clearly tells us that there is nothing new under the sun.

The Anointing of Ease is embedded within God's presence. At a very low point in my life, I prayed this prayer: *"God, I don't feel your presence, but I know you're there. I'm not sure why You won't talk to me or answer me. But every time I try to talk to you, it just turns into complaining. I am so unhappy. I am so disappointed. I am so tired. And right now, nothing good or positive is going to come out of my mouth. Honestly, I don't want to praise You, and I don't feel like prayer works; and this all feels like a waste of time. I'm scared, and I feel like I'm in trouble—because I'm not so sure I'm saved anymore. I need you to tell someone else to pray for me until I can get myself together and come into Your presence the way you require me to; in a way that honors and blesses you. I'm sorry; forgive me, but right now, I need Your help. Amen."*

Those words changed everything. Truthfully, my situation did not immediately improve. The dark cloud that was hanging over my head did not suddenly disappear; but what I did experience was an overwhelming sense of calm and peace that God had heard every word I said. He understood, and He cared. In my spirit I knew that in time, everything was going to work out in ways I couldn't even imagine. I wasn't the first person who had felt that way, and I wouldn't be the last. I knew deep down that 'This too will pass.' If you're going through something right now that seems unbearable and insurmountable, close your eyes, then take a deep breath and whisper aloud: "This too will pass. There is no situation I'm facing that is bigger than God. No matter what happens, I will continue to rest in the assurance of His Word—that all things are working together for my good. For that reason, I will continue to give thanks. It is well with my soul."

Over the years, countless lessons have been learned and shared from my life's experiences. For example, you don't need to have all the answers in advance—no one does. You simply need to start asking the right questions, and then the answers will appear. Questions like: Who do I want to be? How do I want to make a contribution to this world? What problems can I help solve? What do I do well? What difference can I make that matters? Those are the questions to ask.

Along life's journey, there will be mistakes and disappointments—maybe even a bit of discouragement. But that's OK. Those are simply the dues and the price you pay to gain wisdom, knowledge, experience, and success. Everything you need to be successful, you already have inside, along with the indwelling Holy Spirit to instruct and guide you. Every additional bit of knowledge, information, and experience brings you closer to the realization and manifestation of the person you're destined to be. God created you in His image and fashioned you to be a reflection of all that is good. You were not created to be a partial being; you were created to be a whole being, fully equipped with everything you need to be everything you are called to be.

Individual / Group Discussion Question:

In what ways do you make "people pleasing" a priority in your life?

1. _____
2. _____
3. _____
4. _____
5. _____

Notes:

_____
_____
_____
_____

Book Club Discussion Prompts:

O **Why do we care so much about what other people think?**

○ Why do we often value the opinions of people more than we value the opinion of God, our heavenly Father?

○ If you knew without a doubt that the answer would be 'Yes,' and you were guaranteed success, what dreams and goals would you pursue?

Notes:

Anointed to Pray... and to Serve

I once read: "You have the anointing of God flowing through you when God's heart touches another person's heart through your heart. The anointing of God is the presence and guidance of His Holy Spirit. He flows as a river of love, from the throne of grace, through the hearts of believers; bringing life to all that receive His touch." The anointing of God on someone's life is evident because it is not about the person, but all about God and His Spirit moving through them to accomplish something beautiful, wonderful, and majestic.

Think about a worship song that a soloist leads. At first, it's just a song; musical notes in a melody with familiar lyrics. But then something happens, and it becomes much more than a song. It's more than words put to music. The song becomes a healing balm to a wounded heart; comfort to a lonely soul. The song ministers in a way that words alone never could. That's when we recognize that it's not the song or the singer, but the presence of God in the form of His Spirit that has made all the difference.

The anointing is one of those things that rarely gets defined. We talk about it, rejoice because of it; but do we really know what it is, how it moves, and how to access it? Is everyone born with a certain anointing to do certain things? Can you lose your anointing? How is the anointing of God gained or lost? What are you anointed to do?

The passage of Scripture found in Luke 4:18-19, KJV provides a bit of clarity. It reads: "The spirit of the Lord is upon me, because he hath anointed me to preach the gospel to the poor; he hath sent me to heal the brokenhearted, to preach deliverance to the captives, and recovering of sight to the blind, to set at liberty them that are bruised, to preach the acceptable year of the Lord." The NIV reads: "The Spirit of the Lord is on me, because he has anointed me to preach good news to the poor. He has sent me to proclaim freedom for the prisoners and recovery of sight for the blind, to release the oppressed, to proclaim the year of the Lord's favor." By studying those passages of Scripture, we are introduced to five purposes of the anointing:

a. To enable you to "preach the good news" effectively—the good news about Jesus and His redemptive work on the cross. The anointing enables His followers to share it with impact and lasting effect.

b. To make you a messenger, a "proclaimer of freedom" for the prisoners—those imprisoned to sin, drugs, depression, and life-draining habits.

c. To bring "recovery of sight for the blind," enabling both natural and spiritual healing in the lives of others.

d. To empower you to "release the oppressed"— those beaten down and in despair from life.

e. To "proclaim the year of the Lord's favor" and to share the comforting message of God's grace.

As a born-again believer, the anointing of God is available to you because the Holy Spirit is an indwelling presence in you. People are anointed for varying and different reasons, ministries, callings, and situations.

Upon returning from a 2009 missions trip to eastern Africa, someone inquired about the living conditions and bathing conditions there. They asked, "Didn't it bother you that you were dirty and couldn't take a bath in hot water every day?" My response was: "No, because we were all 'dirty' together. What difference would it make if I was clean?" I understood then and now that I was called to serve the people of that region. I was not there to showcase my hygiene or show off my clean clothes. It's the same lesson we learn from the Apostle Paul in 1

Corinthians 9:22, to 'become all things to all people so that through all means, we might save some.'

The anointing allows and enables you to see past the circumstances and look directly toward God's purpose and perfect will for your life. The anointing equips us to accomplish and complete the work we are called to do.

DO YOUR PRAYERS MEET GOD'S EXPECTATIONS?

When preparing to pray, ask yourself the following questions:

1. Will the thing that I am praying for meet my godly personal needs, and will it fit in with a just and righteous lifestyle; or is it self-serving and motivated by self?
2. Am I being submissive to God's will, and will I gladly accept whatever God provides?
3. Is my spirit one of absolute submission to God's holy will?
4. Can I honestly say, 'Not my will, Father, but thy will be done?'
5. Does what I'm praying for honor and glorify God?
6. Does my prayer seek to harm or hurt someone else for my benefit?
7. Will my prayer please God and serve the greater good?
8. Does my prayer request or petition in any way conflict with the Word of God?
9. Do the results of my prayer advance my spiritual growth and spiritual life?
10. Am I taking time to listen; does my time in prayer strengthen my relationship and bring me closer to God?

Individual / Group Discussion Question:

What are you anointed to do for God's kingdom?

1. _____

2. _____

3. _____

4. _____

5. _____

Notes:

_____

_____

_____

_____

_____

Book Club Discussion Prompts:

○ What are your natural strengths, talents, and gifts?

○ What prevents you from using your gifts to bless others?

○ Name the areas of your life where you consistently help others and contribute in a meaningful and positive way.

○ List your Top 5 spiritual gifts and put them into practice on a daily basis.

1._____

2._____

3._____

4._____

5._____

P3 = Privileged-People Problems

There's a Western world phenomenon known as P3, or Privileged-People Problems. It's routinely defined by whiny complaints and dissatisfaction with materialistic things that the majority of the world's population will never possess. P3 petitions are easily identifiable by statements such as: "My _____ (fill in the blank with anything that money can buy) is _____ (fill in the blank with any negative adjective or phrase). Ex. My wardrobe is outdated. Ex. My vacation was too short. You get the idea...

The problem with P3 is that the underlying root cause is pride—defined as haughty, arrogant behavior or exaggerated self-esteem—which is the earth's original sin. Any problem rooted in sin is displeasing to God and therefore must be uprooted and cast away. One of the reasons for the apparent lack of power, faith, and anointing in the body of Christ is that Privileged-People Problems have been mistaken for needs instead of wants, creating an expectation of entitlement.

Immersion in the Anointing of Ease requires a complete and unequivocal release and detachment from natural and material things. That means that there cannot be anything in life that you are not willing to abandon or walk away from in accordance to God's will. Think Abraham's sacrifice of Isaac, the widow's sacrifice of her last mite, the virgin Mary's sacrifice of her reputation and free will, and Jesus' sacrifice of everything.

"And the Lord said unto Gideon, The people that are with thee are too many for me to give the Midianites into their hands, lest Israel vaunt themselves against me saying, Mine own hand hath saved me" (Judges 7:2, KJV). Gideon was preparing for war and facing a lopsided battle in which he appeared doomed. God gave Gideon instructions to test the soldiers and reduce the size of his army. Isn't that just like God; to decrease the army when it's already out-numbered? Gideon's army started with 32,000 men; of them, 22,000 were proven to be afraid, which left 10,000. The 10,000 were told to get a drink of water. Only those who lapped water from hand to mouth were allowed to stay. Out of 10,000, only 300 passed God's test; less than 1 percent.

Gideon witnessed God remove the excess from a situation to secure victory and demonstrate His glory. How will you react when God begins to remove the excess? To put it into relevant context, out of 100 people whom you've met or known throughout your life, only one of them may be crucial to your destiny. Based on this biblical scenario, less than 1 percent of the people you know and the resources you have are needed to divinely receive the miracle or access the blessings you desire in your life. Everything else is extra. In this passage of Scripture, the odds Gideon faced represented less than a 1 percent chance of success. But the story proves that 99 percent of what he had was unnecessary and would not help him win the battle. In reality, all Gideon needed was the Word and Anointing of God to claim victory in battle. It's no different for you and me.

To express dissatisfaction or disappointment to God regarding the outcome of a situation is to elevate your will and desire over the Father's perfect will. When we decide that we know better than God, we essentially default back to the original sin of pride, which was on full display in the Garden of Eden. Spiritual punditry— evidenced by spiritual know-it-alls—is a form of idolatry, because the creation has been exalted above the Creator.

To fully experience the Anointing of Ease requires full surrender and complete faith and reliance on God, and an unwavering trust that His plans are in your eternal best interest. The person or possession that you're unwilling to release is the idol that has the power and ability to hold you hostage and divert your destiny.

Individual / Group Discussion Question:

What things do I regularly complain about?

1. _____
2. _____
3. _____
4. _____
5. _____

If prompted by God's will, is there anything in my life that I am unwilling to walk away from? Why?

1. _____
2. _____
3. _____
4. _____
5. _____

Book Club Discussion Prompts:

○ Why are so many of us inclined to complain, even when we have so much more than others?

○ What does complaining actually accomplish in life?

○ How has ingratitude or ungratefulness affected your life?

○ Is there something you're unwilling to release that is holding you hostage?

Notes:

Be Still and Know...

What is it with this American obsession toward busyness? Have you noticed how many people are overcommitted and super-busy, yet accomplishing little to nothing? Sometimes it seems as though people are in a competition to see who's busier and more exhausted. Honestly, that should not be a race you want to win. The real focus should be on how effective you are, not how busy you are. If you look around and pay attention, it seems like most people are really just "busy doing nothing."

My husband says that I am "efficient." I think that's a compliment—doesn't really matter though, because it's the truth. I am efficient—on purpose. I consistently find a way to accomplish the absolute most with the least amount of effort, energy, and resources. In my mind, there's always an answer, and there's always an easier way; and it's not going to take a very long time to figure out either one. Here are the words I live by: "Get it done." Plus, God already said that I could 'cast my cares upon Him because He cares for me.' In other words, God cares about what I care about; which again, means that God cares about what you care about.

There's an insightful quote that says, "Everyone should strive to generate light, not heat." We are called to be a light unto the world, not to add more negativity and heated discord to an already chaotic scene. We can use our words, our power, our energy, and our resources to be a source of productive, guiding, and reassuring light. Consider the fact that it takes less energy to simply apologize than it does to start, engage, or elevate an argument. It takes less emotional energy to allow someone to cut into your lane of traffic than it does to fight over the space for an extended period of time. It takes less energy to say, 'No, thank you. I'm not able to do that' than it does to make up 10 different excuses, and explain and rationalize why you would like to do something, but aren't sure you can, but will try your best to fit it in. Why??? Say what you mean, and mean what you say. And if what you mean is 'No,' then just say it.

The Anointing of Ease will allow you to give yourself and others a break. It doesn't mean that you become a pushover, and it doesn't mean that you don't stand up for yourself when necessary. But it does mean that you let some things go, because they simply aren't worth your time. It does mean that you don't always have to be heard and get the last word. It does mean that you pick your battles carefully and don't spend major time on minor issues.

"No, thank you" is a complete sentence. It has a subject, a verb, and an object. It also requires no explanation. Years ago, I received a call from a credit card company offering me an "amazing" interest rate and a discount on my next summer vacation. "No, thank you" was my answer. The pitch from the representative sounded something like this: "Ma'am, are you saying that you don't want to save money? Are you saying that you don't want to take advantage of this amazing deal and this great opportunity? If you don't act now, you will miss out on an incredible deal. Are you saying that you're willing to miss out on this?" My response, "No, thank you." And then he hung up. No reasoning, no rationalizing, no apologizing, and no explaining. Why? Because, 'No, thank you' is a complete sentence.

Not too long ago, a friend of mine was talking about how she didn't have time to clean up her home. She was exhausted from the full-time duties of being a working wife and mother, and volunteer. I simply suggested hiring a housecleaning service; not for a year, not every week, but for one day. The idea was simple: You're tired right now, and you're very busy. You don't have to figure out everything for the next month or the next year. Just get through the day. You've worked hard. Budget for what you want done, and then give yourself a break. No matter how much it costs (not a lot), it will still be less than physically, mentally, and emotionally burning yourself out because you feel like you need to do everything yourself. Ask for help when you need it, and don't stop asking until you get it. Once we're willing to release the fallacy that 'no one can clean my house like me' or whatever it might be, we can freely accept assistance and the easier solutions that come our way.

The Difference a Day Makes

If you can change one thing, you can change anything; if you can change anything, then you can change everything. Almost 10 years ago, I decided to undergo the 24-Hour Transformation. It's a formula for changing the trajectory of your life. I understood this harsh reality: If you are dissatisfied with any area of your life, it is most likely your own fault. However, there is good news. Literally, all it takes is one defining moment and one different decision to take the necessary action and steps toward the life you desire.

One morning I woke up and made a commitment to create the life I really wanted; not the life other people wanted for me or the life society suggested was most appropriate for me. I made a decision to change my mind, and it changed my life. The premise of the 24-Hour Transformation is based solely on the difference a day makes. It literally takes one day (sometimes, just one moment) to change your life for the better—or for the worse. The choice is ours.

The 24-Hour Transformation can be a literal 24-hour day or a progressive philosophical series of steps that equate to a cerebral shift in how you think about and live your life. Keep in mind, 24 hours is one way, but it's not the only way. But for me, it was the best way. In one day, I stepped into a life defined by the Anointing of Ease—quick, fast, and in a hurry.

When I think of the Anointing of Ease, I envision stepping out of the bubble of life as we know it and into a parallel universe that more closely reflects life the way God originally ordained it to be. There is always the option to step back inside the bubble, only to find it limiting and suffocating. Life outside the bubble is better.

The Anointing of Ease can often be mistaken for individual effort or ability. Yes, the Bible tells us there is profit in all labor. However, there are limits to the doors that labor alone can open. It makes a big difference to have the anointing on your side. The beauty of God's anointing is that it always works, even when our individual efforts fall short.

On a Thursday morning in February 2007, I woke up feeling awful. After a couple of doctor's appointments that week and the next, I received a call on my cell phone. The nurse on the other end asked an unexpectedly direct question: "Miss Fields, are you prepared to have a hysterectomy?" (I was only in my 20s; still single and childless). I sat speechless in my car, unable to comprehend how my life had changed so drastically in a matter of days. A week later, I was rushed to the emergency room. My lower abdomen had swollen to three times its normal size, and the level of pain was excruciating. I groaned in agony in the waiting room and holding rooms at the hospital for 10 hours before going into surgery. I awakened in a recovery room surrounded by family members. I wasn't sure if I was going to live or if I was going to die. Everyone looked stunned. As the anesthesia and grogginess wore off, I began to hear different versions of what happened. I had undergone surgery to have a fibroid tumor the size of a 5-month-old fetus removed. The tumor had twisted in my abdomen, which is what caused the pain. The fibroid was filled with blood vessels and was essentially draining the blood and life out of me, which is what caused the initial symptoms of my illness.

The doctor came in my room to report that my tumor had grown on a stalk (like a plant) that allowed the surgeons to easily remove it without disturbing or removing any of my reproductive organs. I was told I had two healthy ovaries still intact. During my surgery, there was minimal bleeding, minimal scarring, and I was told I could expect a speedy recovery.

Unfortunately, my medical insurance had expired and was not reinstated prior to my emergency room visit. While at home recovering, I received a bill for $18,000; a relative fortune for me, but an amount I considered a small price to pay for my life.

There were two ways to look at my situation. I chose to see the good because I knew that God was bigger than my circumstances. I (and my prayer warriors) praised God for a successful surgery. I thanked Him for healing my body and restoring me to health. Every day, I quietly meditated and worshipped in His presence and basked in a realization that the enemy had tried and failed to physically take me out of here—understanding and experiencing like never before the passage from Isaiah 54:17, which declares that 'no weapon formed against me will prosper.'

As my health improved and I regained some independence, my initial response was to try to handle everything on my own. That's what the spirit of pride encourages us to do—to act like a one-person army. However, it immediately became clear that I was too tired (mentally and physically), and too broke (financially), to handle my situation alone. I didn't want to ask for help, but I needed to ask for help. More than anything, I needed to realize that the answers I sought were already in place, just awaiting the moment for me to put aside my pride and accept that God was going to bless me and answer my prayer through others.

During my recovery, I didn't have all the answers; I didn't even know all the questions, but I was grateful to God, and I learned to BE STILL. My small business continued to grow (without me); my sisters prayed for, cared for, and cooked for me; my father moved into my home to help take care of me, and over the next several weeks, my body healed perfectly.

And then it came. A letter from the hospital arrived in the mail stating that the balance of my $18,000 medical bill was $0. I had yet to make a single payment. To this day, I do not know how the bill was paid, other than the grace of God, which is sufficient to cover any cost. In my life, in more ways than one, Jesus literally paid it all. That's the Anointing of Ease at work.

The Anointing of Ease balances the scales of Suffering and Surrender in life. For where there is no brokenness, there is no potential for healing and restoration, and there rarely is complete submission. Prior to the Anointing in my life, there had been hurt, disappointment, doubt, and depression. There was anger and frustration with God, along with a shocking realization of my refusal and inability to completely trust His plan for my life.

"God, where are you?" I cried from the depths of my soul. "What kind of Father treats His child like this?" This moment of despair was reflective of an Old Testament conversation not unlike the one Job had with God during his tumultuous tribulation. Out of hurt, frustration, and desperation, I cried: "God, I trusted you. I begged and pleaded with you. I have prayed and fasted and tried to do everything you've asked me to do. What about all the people who don't even acknowledge You? How is it their lives are better than mine?" God responded with silence. I was lost and furious. God said nothing; because He acts according to our faith; not our fears, our tears, or our frustration.

When I stopped struggling and straining—and offered my life in full surrender—something miraculous happened. Everything changed for the better. The blessings in my life ushered in by the Anointing of Ease came effortlessly. There was no labor or travail in prayer, no begging or pleading in desperation. There was simply a decree; a declaration of what God's Word already confirmed, along with a confident assurance in the ability to call forth those things that be not as though they were.

You Are Not Alone... Never Have Been, Never Will Be

For anyone who has ever felt like they were all alone and that they couldn't go on... you can, and you will. During my dark days of hopeless contemplation, I wanted to know my options. I sat at my computer and I entered a search term on "suicide" to consider the various ways to end it all. A website page opened with this phrase: If you are considering suicide click here. I clicked the button and here's what appeared on the next screen: 'Suicide is a permanent solution for a temporary problem. God loves you! Please accept Jesus in your heart today.' I almost fell out of my chair. At the point where I thought no one could find me, there He was...

watching and waiting and welcoming me back home. And there along with me was the Anointing of Ease that allowed me to know the reality of God's presence and experience the inevitability of His Will—even when I didn't know it, believe it, or like it. My life lesson from that experience is this: At the end of you, there is God.

Are there areas of your life where you can admit that you need help and support? *'You have not, because you ask not; ask and you will receive.'*

- O　　Spiritual Growth/Spiritual Guidance
- O　　Mental Health/Therapy
- O　　Domestic Support, Housework & Chores
- O　　Budgeting and Financial Planning
- O　　Family Counseling
- O　　Skills Assessment/Job Training
- O　　Domestic Violence/Abuse/Sexual Assault
- O　　Sexuality/Temptation
- O　　Alcoholism/Addiction
- O　　Drug/Substance Abuse
- O　　Depression/Loneliness/Suicidal Thoughts
- O　　Post-Traumatic Stress Disorder
- O　　Post-Partum Depression
- O　　Body Image/Eating Disorders

Resources

American Association of Christian Counselors
www.aacc.net

Christian Credit Counselors
www.ChristianCreditCounselors.org

Crown Financial Ministries
www.crown.org

Focus on the Family (Christian Counseling Referrals)
www.FocusOnTheFamily.com

National Institute of Mental Health
www.nimh.nih.gov

National Sexual Assault Hotline
(800) 656-HOPE (4673)

National Suicide Prevention Lifeline
(800) 273-TALK (8255)

RAINN (Rape, Abuse & Incest National Network)
www.rainn.org

Substance Abuse and Mental Health Services Administration
(800) 662-HELP (4357)

U.S. Department of Health & Human Services
www.MentalHealth.gov

4th Quarter ~ Ease on Down the Road

Promises, Promises...

Over the years I've discovered there is a general misunderstanding about the gift of salvation and the gifts of salvation. The redemptive work of Christ on the Cross laid the groundwork for salvation, which is a free gift from God—that we cannot or could not earn or deserve. The gifts and promises of God throughout our lives are conditional—predicated by our willingness and ability to walk according to His Word to fulfill His will. Based on Scripture, we know that the promises of God are IN HIM, meaning the recipients are walking and living in accordance to the Word and will of God; positioned in "right standing" with God through Christ, and maintaining a spiritual relationship through acceptance of His Son Jesus as Lord and Savior.

The simple truth: Salvation is a gift. It is freely offered as an expression of love through the sacrificial death of God's Son—Christ the Messiah and Savior of the world. Salvation cannot be earned because its value is immeasurable.

Each year millions of people eagerly embrace the bondage of religion, doctrine, dogma, and tradition in an attempt to earn the benefit of God's love; attempting to pay a price they simply can't afford. People struggle to be good enough, faithful enough, loyal enough; and continually fall short of a goal they are not equipped to achieve.

The irony of these futile attempts is that they are unnecessary. There has never been an expectation for people to earn salvation because it is a gift from God. Scripture clearly indicates that Jesus' death, burial, and resurrection were the fulfillment of the law.

The Anointing of Ease is in direct proportion to the Spirit of Release. The more you let go, the easier life becomes. In this society there is too much of everything, which is a breeding ground for greed, waste, and ungratefulness. It's time to release and let go of some things to make room for the anointing and to remember who we are in God's providential plan.

"All the paths of the LORD are mercy and truth unto such as keep his covenant and his testimonies. For thy name's sake, O LORD, pardon mine iniquity; for it is great. What man is he that feareth the LORD? him shall he teach in the way that he shall choose. **His soul shall dwell at ease;** and his seed shall inherit the earth" (Psalm 25:10-13, KJV). **Reverence the Lord, and your soul shall dwell at ease.** "Thus saith the LORD unto you, Be not afraid nor dismayed by reason of this great multitude; for the battle is not yours, but God's" (2 Chronicles 20:15b, KJV). This is a reminder that our position and perspective in life is from a Victory Vantage-point, where we always triumph in Christ Jesus. Here's an easy analogy to keep things in perspective.

Life is like a play. The mistake that many people make in life is playing the wrong part. The script has been written, and it flows much more smoothly when all the actors, characters, and players stick to their assigned roles. In the screenplay of your life, you are the central character, a flawed—yet likeable—individual who faces ups, downs, challenges, triumphs, overwhelming conflict, an adversary, and a moment of truth. Satan, the enemy of your soul is the antagonist, whose role is to attack, assault, and continually accuse the main character. There are extras, crowd scenes, changing sets and backgrounds, and random bit players who help to make or break a scene. Also there is Providence, the overarching guiding principle of good; and there is a protagonist, the hero of the story, featuring the Father, Son, and Holy Spirit—appearing and starring as the Holy Trinity.

Plays and scripts don't work when a character speaks the wrong lines or forgets her/his role. Everything that the enemy says from the script will be a lie, designed to deceive and mislead the main character. Your role is to 'cast your cares on God, for he cares for you.' Study the Bible to memorize your lines and speak only words of truth, provided in the holy text. These words are God's promises: words of truth, power, peace, love, faith, forgiveness, healing, deliverance, and victory. God will do the rest. He will order your steps, fight your battles, direct your paths, protect your way, hide you in the safety of his wings of refuge, love you unconditionally, forgive your sins, deliver you from evil, restore your soul, give you rest, and freely offer the gift of eternal life. He will give you victory, peace, and a life of anointed ease. "Surely goodness and mercy shall follow me all the days of my life: and I will dwell in the house of the Lord forever" (Psalm 23:6, KJV). When you are where you're supposed to be—doing what you're supposed to be doing and saying what you're supposed to be saying— good things and mercy will find you and follow you for your entire life. That is the Anointing of Ease at work.

Depending upon which Bible scholar you ask, there are literally thousands of promises that God has made to mankind. The Bible clearly tells us in James 4:2-3 that 'you have not, because you ask not; and when you do ask, you don't receive because you ask with the wrong motives.' How many people are guilty of that?

Unfortunately, many of us are missing out on greatness because we simply don't know God's promises—and what rightly belongs to us. Once you learn what promises have been made, you can pray with a renewed sense of purpose and authority to manifest the perfect will of God in your life.

In 2 Corinthians 1:20 we learn: "For all the promises of God in him are yea, and in him Amen, unto the glory of God by us." And like many other spiritual concepts, the promises are conditional, meaning to get God's promises, you must do things God's way.

Here's another way to think about it. For those of you who are parents or guardians, who do you provide for? The people in your house. We generally don't work hard and pay bills to take care of random people whom we don't know—who are not a part of our household. Strangers from the neighborhood can't just show up at your house and start making demands about what they want, what they deserve, and what you should give them. It doesn't work that way.

In the same way, if we're outside the household of faith—living by the devil's rules—we have no right to make a claim or make demands of God and then expect Him to fulfill them. Next, if we're living in contradiction to God's Word, we can have no expectation for His promises. Although God is faithful, our sin will separate us from Him and cause a 'breach of contract' between us and His promises. Active sin in our lives weakens our faith, and without faith, it is impossible to please God.

To paraphrase, the Bible says that God has "given to us exceedingly great and precious promises" (2 Peter 1:4). Consider Psalm 37:4, "Delight yourself also in the LORD, and He shall give you the desires of your heart" and "If you abide in Me, and My words abide in you, you will ask what you desire, and it shall be done for you" (John 15:7). Other wonderful promises include: "If we confess our sins, He is faithful and just to forgive us our sins and to cleanse us from all unrighteousness" (1 John 1:9); "The steps of a good man are ordered by the LORD, and He delights in his way. Though he fall, he shall not be utterly cast down; for the LORD upholds him with His hand" (Psalm 37:23-24). The Bible also tells us that Jesus is "the way, the truth, and the life" and that "no one comes to the Father except through Him" (John 14:6). So, if we want to be heard by God and want to receive His promises, the conditions are clear. The Word tells us that "He who promised is faithful." God cannot lie; what He promises, He is also able to perform. God is good. God is great. God is faithful.

Focus on 'What Is,' not 'What If'

On any given day, a thousand different things could potentially go wrong. Such is the nature of our lives. However, no one can predict the future, so it's better to simply focus on what you have in front of you instead of allowing your imagination to conjure up what might potentially happen. In business, we often say that a good plan today is better than a perfect plan tomorrow.

In life it is easier to focus on 'what is' instead of trying to figure out answers to the countless 'what ifs.' Years ago, a study on mental health indicated that approximately 80 percent of the things we worry about never happen. Think about how inefficient and wasteful it is to spend precious time focusing on something that never actually occurs. What else could you accomplish with an extra 80 percent of your time each day?

As a rule, I am very decisive. Meaning, I make informed decisions and then I don't second-guess them. I've learned to get things done in that manner by focusing on 'what is' rather than 'what if.' When it's time to make a decision, my process is to collect all of the information that is available to me, factor in all of the opinions that are relevant to the decision I need to make, and then rely on prayer for guidance, and my God-given ability to rightly apply knowledge and achieve wisdom.

For me, it's a formula that works—like Wash. Rinse. Repeat. My confidence has grown in this area because my faith and trust in God's guidance have grown also. Basically, all of my trust is in God. I know that His Spirit is in me, so the only voice I hear is His. I want to share with you this very simple lesson in faith.

When I was about 5 years old, my father took me and my two older sisters to the community swimming pool to teach me how to swim. He was standing in waist-deep water, and I was standing on the edge of the pool. My father said to me, "Jump!" I stood on the edge of the pool, looking at him like he was crazy. "Jump?!?" You can't be serious. "*What if* you don't catch me?" I asked. He said, "I'll catch you, but you have to jump in." After a few back and forth exchanges that ended with me not jumping, I finally jumped. And, lo and behold, he caught me. It was easier to jump the next time, and the time after that, because his track record of catching me was perfect, and because my confidence in his ability to catch me grew. Here's the lesson I figured out some 25 years later: My father was not going to let me drown, because he loved me, and I was (am) precious to him. And not only that, it also dawned on me that my father was standing on the bottom of the pool. He was not struggling to stand up or stay afloat. He was well-grounded and his balance was rock-solid. In that pool scenario, the only thing that was uncertain was me.

Now, let's apply that lesson to contemporary life. Your Heavenly Father is not going to let you drown. He loves you, and you are precious to Him. Not only that, the Creator is standing on the bottom (of everything). He is well-grounded and His balance is rock solid. The only thing that is uncertain is you. You are the 'what if,' but God represents 'What Is.'

If you've ever had to wait on God to do something, then you know firsthand that it can be difficult, agonizing, and frustrating. And because our eternal God transcends time and space, He is rarely in a hurry.

The Anointing of Ease is built on the practices of trusting in the Word of God and resting in the arms of God. Once you make up your mind that however God chooses to touch your life, you will be satisfied, then things get a whole lot easier. Once we decide to stop whining, complaining, worrying, agonizing, and being in a perpetual state of frustration; once we decide to put a situation in God's hands and leave it there; once we decide that, 'Though He slay me, yet will I trust Him," and once we understand that God's ways and thoughts are not our ways and thoughts; and that His ways and thoughts are higher and better, then the result will be an open door into the Anointing of Ease. It is that level of faith to which God responds, which also ushers in the atmosphere for blessings, miracles, and answered prayers.

No matter what is going on in your life—no matter how dark the situation may seem—God is on your side; and you are not alone because somebody, somewhere is praying for you. Not only that, God has given His angels charge over you; the Holy Spirit is making intercession for you; Jesus Christ, the Son of God, is seated at the right hand of the Father in heaven praying for you. The fact is, that when you're in Christ, you are never alone. You have not been forgotten, and you will not be forsaken.

Here is a very clear example from the second book of Kings, Chapter 6, beginning at verse 15 (NIV): "When the servant of the man of God got up and went out early the next morning, an army with horses and chariots had surrounded the city. 'Oh my Lord, what shall we do,' the servant asked. 'Don't be afraid,' the prophet answered. Those who are with us are more than those who are with them.' And Elisha prayed, 'Oh Lord, open his eyes so he may see.' Then the Lord opened the servant's eyes, and he looked and saw the hills full of horses and chariots of fire all around Elisha."

There are two main points that can be gleaned from that passage. The first is that the help we need is already here because God promised to never leave us nor forsake us; just because you don't see something, doesn't mean it's not there. The second point is that somebody else is always praying and interceding on your behalf. Notice, the servant didn't pray for himself at first. Elisha recognized that the servant was worried and fearful, and Elisha then interceded on his behalf—and God answered the prayer promptly. For a moment, God allowed the invisible to become visible, and He allowed the supernatural to intersect with the natural. The bottom line though is that whether God had allowed Elisha and the servant to see the surrounding chariots or not, they were still there, protecting His people and doing the will of God—that's why His people can feel at ease and focus on 'what is.'

In Romans 8:26 (NIV), we learn, "In the same way, the Spirit helps us in our weakness. We do not know what we ought to pray for, but the Spirit himself intercedes for us with groans that words cannot express. And he who searches our hearts knows the mind of the Spirit, because the Spirit intercedes for the saints in accordance with God's will."

Navigating day-to-day life in the Anointing of Ease requires patience—even while operating in faith. We are given model directions in prayer to only request, "Give us this day, our daily bread" (Matthew 6:11, KJV). In general, this is a struggle because it leaves so much room for uncertainty—in essence, it requires the petitioner to give up some (if not all) control. "Give us this day, our daily bread" limits and defines our asking. We are not led to pray about future unknown situations and circumstances ('what ifs'), or to launch a preemptive strike against the evil forces of the world, or to generate a list of wishes that would result in a pain-free, problem-free existence—void of trials and adversity. "Give us this day, our daily bread" means that our focus needs to be on taking one day at a time; and that believers should consistently look to God as the source of provision. If we make the commitment to focus on 'What Is,' God will handle all of the 'What Ifs.'

What if this is the answer to my prayers? What if he is the one? What if this man is my future husband?

At age 34, I met the man of my dreams. It's a bit of a cliché, but he was 'tall, dark, and handsome.' We had similar childhoods, we liked the same things, and we really enjoyed spending time together. For me, he was the answer to prayer I had been waiting for. I hoped and prayed that he felt the same way.

Over a period of weeks, then months, then years, we continued to get closer. First friends, and then really good friends. We chatted on the phone every week, exchanged email messages, and went out to lunch together. I prayed for confirmation from God that this was the relationship I had been waiting for. At that time, I felt that God wanted me to know He would demonstrate His love for me through this new earthly love. The relationship with my friend was innocent, sweet, and beautiful. He never said or did anything too forward or inappropriate, which made me all the more hopeful that what we had shared together thus far was a positive indication of what the future would bring.

I waited for the next level of our relationship to arrive, but it never did. We just kept being very good friends. I prayed for guidance on what to say and what to do; to feel confident that I was appealing and attractive to him. It didn't seem to make a difference. Over time, I became frustrated; then disappointed; and then devastated.

One particular Monday morning, he called me just to say hello—and to share some news. Within the first minute of our conversation, he also told me that he was engaged and planning to get married the following year. I was stunned.

I didn't miss a beat in my response: "Oh my goodness! Congratulations—I had no idea." That was all I could say with any level of sincerity. We talked for another few minutes. Rather, he talked about his recent proposal while I tried to fake interest and excitement for his happiness. After we hung up, I leaned back in the chair and tried to hold back my tears.

Oddly enough, I was happy for my friend because he seemed genuinely happy. But I was furious at God for not answering my prayer and for allowing me to get my hopes up, when He knew what was going to happen all along.

As my friend's wedding day approached, I sank deeper into the sad realization of what would never be. Our friendship took a backseat to his new life, and we gradually lost touch completely. On occasion someone would mention his name, but our paths never crossed again.

For months, I wrestled with the disappointment and hurt feelings of losing a love that I thought I had found. Eventually the sadness I felt turned to confusion, which descended into numbness—that over time, hardened my heart. "God, how did I miss you on this one? How could this happen? What did I do wrong? I thought that you were going to show Your love for me through my love and marriage to him. This hurts so badly, I'm not sure my heart will ever heal."

Time moved on and so did I. Somewhat grudgingly, I followed my own advice and told myself, "Well, if you won't get over it, at least get on with it." There were still some unanswered questions in the back of my mind, but I reconciled my single life with the justification that it just simply wasn't meant to be. I convinced myself that if the worst problem I had was a broken heart, then things really weren't that bad at all.

Like with anything, time heals all wounds. I discovered new ways to enjoy my life and continued pursuing goals and dreams that were of interest to me. I continued living a wonderful life and moved on.

Several years later, the news showed up in my email in-box out of nowhere. My friend was sick. Before I was able to fully find out and comprehend what was happening, the news came that my friend was dead.

The former lost-love with whom I once had hoped to share my life had died.

I grieved for his loss. I prayed for his family. I recalled memories from years past of the wonderful friendship we had and the time we spent together. And then I acknowledged something I had not considered before: Yes, I was sad to lose a friend; but I was spared from having to bury my husband.

Of course, there was no way I could have known all those years earlier that my friend would die before he reached the age of 42. But God knew the end of the story from the beginning, and He demonstrated His tremendous love for me by protecting me from a tragedy that would take years to unfold.

Armed only with my limited information and short-sighted objective to have a relationship, I arrived at an incorrect conclusion about what my life should be. Fortunately, God's sufficient grace and omniscience preceded and protected me from a threat I didn't even know was there. I realized that God never wavered in His promises to me; He protected and loved me unconditionally—when it appeared to hurt and discourage me—even when I didn't understand. All along, He had something (and someone) wonderful for me, and all that was required was that I trust in His will for my life.

The Power of Agreement:

For those who are willing to pursue them, at the intersection of Acceptance and Agreement you will find perfect Peace and Ease.

Agreement is one of the core foundational principles of salvation in Scripture; hence, it is the building block of our lives and the platform on which the Anointing of Ease stands.

Agreement is a coming together of the minds. Agreement is focus, mission, and purpose linked to a common goal. Agreement strengthens power by combining ability. When our lives line up with God's Word and are in agreement with His will, life becomes a whole lot easier.

The strongest agreement that we can have is oneness with the Word of God. When our lives, attitudes, and prayers line up with the Word, answered prayer is easy. The reason that all of Jesus' prayers were answered is that His life was in agreement with the will of God, the Father. And because Jesus is the living Word of God, we know that His life was also synonymous and on one accord with the Word.

It is awe-inspiring to know and understand that the Father, Son, and Holy Spirit are ONE—representing perfect agreement. Many of us struggle in life, in our marriages, in our careers, in our homes, and with our attitudes because we are misaligned and in dis-Agreement with the Word. When we talk about the power of agreement, we're essentially saying that because our lives are in alignment with God's Word and will, that we can fearlessly speak the Word with Power and Authority through our God-given Dominion. Then, according to our faith (in God's ability to bring it to pass), we can expect to receive the desired answers to our prayers.

Agreement in Action

When I agreed to marry my husband, I agreed to accept him as he was—for who he was. He did the same. I was under no disillusionment that I could or would try to change him once we were married. He too accepted and embraced me As-Is; no refunds or exchanges. Now, that doesn't mean that we won't learn, change, grow, and adapt together; however, it does mean that our eyes were wide open to who we were and what we were getting as a result of our union.

Early on, the simplest and best advice I received about marriage was this: Marry the right person. The next best advice was this: Get married in God's timing, not your own. And after that: Get married for the right reasons. To sum it up: Right person. Right timing. Right reasons.

Prior to getting married, my husband and I decided that the focal points of our marriage would be ONENESS and AGREEMENT. To the best of our collective ability, we were going to be one team, operating on one accord, toward one common vision for our newly united lives.

In practice, this means if we are not in agreement, then we are not doing something right, and we will not overlook or ignore that which is wrong. Agreement is our objective, and the decision-making process in our home only leads to agreement. If we disagree about an issue, we cannot move forward until we find a place of common interest, which will lead us to agree on something—one thing, anything. We may not agree on everything, but we cannot proceed until we agree on something. From that united point of agreement, we can pray and seek God's guidance on what to do next. As a couple, we agree that there is one perfect will of God for whatever decision we are making. Consequently, when we both are in agreement with God, we are also in agreement with each other.

In Scripture, Amos 3:3 asks, 'How can two walk together, except they be in agreement?' In simplified terms, if I want red and my husband wants blue, we must both accept red; or both accept blue; or blend our red and blue to create purple. Speaking from a spiritual perspective, in our home, God is the piano, and we are both different instruments in His orchestra. If my husband is a trombone, and I am a flute, when we are both in tune with the Piano, we are in tune with each other and living in spiritual harmony. That is the spirit of agreement and the Anointing of Ease at work, and at play.

Our example for oneness is a simple one: The Father, Son, and Holy Spirit are in such perfect agreement, that they are ONE. Can you imagine it? Life without discord or dis-Agreement? Envision for a moment a life of perfect peace and ease. It is possible, and it is promised. "Thou wilt keep him in **perfect peace**, whose mind is stayed on thee: because he trusteth in thee" (Isaiah 26:3, KJV).

Admittedly, I have not been married long enough to have a tested and tried opinion about it. But, I do know that I never quite understood when I heard countless people say, 'Marriage is hard.' I never really grasped how and why loving someone should be difficult. To be honest, I still don't. Hard marriages appear to stem from one of three things: 1) Wrong person; 2) Wrong timing; 3) Wrong reasons.

By the time I got married in my 40s, I had the benefit of time, experience, age, wisdom, and observation. I was able to watch what a lot of other people got wrong—and then hopefully and prayerfully, get it right. Time will tell.

My husband and I both had been told on many occasions that the first year of marriage was the hardest. Giving people the benefit of the doubt, I'm guessing they meant well and just wanted us to be prepared for the potential difficulties of blending two lives together. However, our first year of marriage was fantastic and wonderful! It was fun-filled with love, joy, peace, passion, happiness, and gratitude for being together. Dare I say it, our first year of marriage was easy! I am confident that the ease we experienced was because of our prior mutual commitment toward acceptance and agreement and a refusal to accept anything less than God's promised best for us.

Not long after our one-year anniversary, a good friend who has been married more than 50 years said to me: "Don't let anyone tell you that things will get worse as time goes on. Things just get better!" I receive it, in Jesus' name—Amen.

Ask yourself this: In marriage or in life, am I willing to give more than I get? Be honest: Am I willing to give more than I get? If you're not willing to give, you'll never be satisfied with what you get. If it helps, make a list with two columns. At the top of one side write, 'What I want to get.' And at the top of the other side, write: 'What I'm willing to give or give up.' And if what you hope to get is longer than what you're willing to give, then you're in for a very rude awakening.

God gave us the perfect example through Christ. Symbolically, in the Bible, the church is the Bride of Christ; and from Genesis to Revelation—and every generation in between—God is basically giving everything and getting nothing in return. The good news is that we already have a much better deal than that one, if we'll only take advantage of it. God's unconditional love for us is not "because of," rather, it is "in spite of."

The Power of Agreement in marriage, in business, in friendships, and in life is a building block of Spiritual Intimacy. Let's further explore how agreement—and its opposite, dis-Agreement—work.

The Six D's of Dis-Ease

There are six terms I want you to remember: Disagreement. Discord. Disobedience. Diminishment. Displeasure. Destruction.

These six terms are connected. Disagreement results in discord. Discord results in disobedience. Disobedience creates sin. Sin diminishes faith. Lack of faith displeases God. Displeasure with God destroys Spiritual Intimacy. One more time. Disagreement results in discord. Discord results in disobedience. Disobedience creates sin. Sin diminishes faith. Lack of faith displeases God. Displeasure with God destroys Spiritual Intimacy.

This lesson goes all the way back to the beginning; back to the book of Genesis in the Garden of Eden with Adam and Eve. God established His word with Adam and Eve and provided very simple and clear instructions. 'Of all the fruit of the trees in the garden, you may eat. But of the fruit of the tree which is in the midst of the garden you shall not eat it, and you shall not touch it, otherwise you will die.' Then the serpent introduces the idea of Disagreement. You can see where it starts in Genesis 3:4. "And the serpent said unto the woman, ye shall not surely die: For God doth know that in the day ye eat thereof, then your eyes shall be as gods, knowing good and evil." Verse 6: "...and when the woman saw that the tree was good for food, and that it was pleasant to the eyes, and a tree to be desired to make one wise, she took of the fruit thereof, and did eat, and gave also unto her husband with her; and he did eat."

Notice in just three verses, we have Disagreement, Discord, and Disobedience; and because of sin, it resulted in a Diminishing of the relationship with God; Displeasure by God; and Destruction of the environment and framework of the relationship that had been in place. At the end of that chapter, in Verse 24, we learn: "So He (God) drove out the man; and He placed at the east of the garden of Eden cherubims, and a flaming sword which turned every way, to keep the way of the tree of life."

It is clear that the path from Dis-Agreement to Destruction is straight and swift. It is also avoidable.

When believers are in correct spiritual alignment, they will experience the Anointing of Ease. If this idea is new to you, there are a few easy ways to start: Prayer. Praise. Worship. Presence. Obedience. Faith. Submission.

Very simply, Prayer is communication with God. You talk, He listens. He talks, you listen. Prayer is a dialogue, not a monologue. If 90 percent of your prayer is talking, and only 10 percent is listening, you're missing out on what God has for you. Think about this: God has every answer to every question or concern you have. He literally told us to cast our cares on Him because He cares for us. That means if you care about something, then God cares about it too, because He cares about you. If you are talking, then you are not listening; and if you are not listening, then you are not learning. You can get more done with 10 words of prayer and an hour in His presence than you'll ever get done begging, crying, pleading, and complaining about what's wrong in your life.

Praise creates an immediate connection with God. We read in the Bible that God inhabits the praises of His people. That means He takes up residence in the words you say that honor Him. God lives in your praise. So when you say 'glory' or 'hallelujah,' which is the highest praise, you have an assurance that God is in the midst. I ministered at a youth conference in Uganda, (east) Africa for four hours (outside under a mango tree) to more than 200 young people who did not speak a word of English. I had a translator with me. But when I said "Jesus" or I said "Hallelujah," they just started smiling and clapping. Jesus and Hallelujah. So, if you cannot think of anything else to say, just call on Jesus and say Hallelujah, and you will get heaven's attention.

Worship is our quiet time to reverence God; to contemplate on His mighty works; and to meditate upon His goodness and marvel at His glory. Worship also ushers us into the Presence of God, where we can witness in our spirits to His majesty. As a believer, when you're in the presence of God, there is nowhere else you desire to be: not at work, not at the office, not at school, not with friends, not at the mall, not on social media. What an honor it is for you to have an invitation to commune with and sit at the feet of the Lord; the Great I AM; the Creator of all that is. What an humbling experience that God would allow us to come into His Presence and spend time with Him; and He simply loves us in return.

Spiritual Intimacy also requires Obedience, which we are told is better than sacrifice. Why Obedience? Because He's God and we're not! It really is that simple. Intimacy also requires Faith, which is trust, reliance, and confidence. Where there is no trust, there is no intimacy. We know from the Bible that without faith, it is impossible to please God.

Spiritual intimacy requires transparency and vulnerability. When we are vulnerable, we expose our weaknesses. It's OK to talk to God about your weaknesses, because He already knows them. But, I wonder how many of you have been open, honest, and vulnerable with yourselves? A lot of us are lying to ourselves. We are telling ourselves that we're OK and that God is pleased with our lives... and He isn't. Many of us aren't even pleased with our own lives. We're in just enough pain to hurt, but not enough to change. So, let's take a closer look at ourselves.

Here's a visual example: If Jesus showed up on your doorstep and you invited Him in, is there anything or any room in your house you wouldn't want Him to see? Are there areas in your spiritual house that are in a state of disarray and dis-Ease that you don't want Him or anybody else to know about?

When He walks in, do you keep Him in the living room because there are dirty dishes and dirty laundry in the kitchen? Or liquor on the countertops? Or marijuana in the cabinets? Or pornography in the drawers of the bedroom? Or gambling sites on the computer? Or text messages from someone else's husband/wife on your smartphone?

Walking successfully in the Anointing of Ease begins with the truth; that means being honest with God and being honest with yourself. When it comes to getting closer to God, ourselves, and each other, we're going to need to come clean and confess some things: James

5:16, KJV says "Confess your faults one to another, and pray one for another, that ye may be healed. The effectual fervent prayer of a righteous man availeth much."

If I can't show God the whole house or my whole heart, then I'm missing out on some things. If I'm afraid to show God my whole heart, then I'm missing out on His best for my life. As a believer and follower of Christ, if I cannot admit that I'm not perfect and that some things may be out of order in my life, then I'm never going to get delivered from them.

Some of us have unforgiveness in our hearts that dates back for years, maybe even decades. We're still hurt, mad, angry, and upset about something. Yes, somebody did us wrong, that is part of how life works. But holding on to unforgiveness is like cutting your hand and expecting the other person to bleed. Unforgiveness in your heart literally works like an acid that's eating you alive from the inside-out. We must forgive, and we must accept forgiveness in order to be free.

For whatever reason, some people are angry with God, but too ashamed to admit it. I know because I've been there, and I know what it looks like and what it feels like. Just know that you are never too far gone for God to reach you; and whom the Son sets free is free indeed. Some years ago, I was ministering at a women's conference. After the session was over, a woman whose son had been murdered came up to me in tears. She said, "Minister Fields, I keep praying and praying and praying, but I just can't seem to make any progress. It's been years since my son was killed, but I'm stuck in the same place." I listened for a few minutes and then I told her what no one else had. I said, "Sister, the problem is that you're mad at God. And that's OK, because He already knows it."

Right then and there, we prayed for forgiveness. She confessed to God that she was angry with Him that He had not protected her child. She had not forgiven the reality that her son had been taken. Then she apologized and asked for forgiveness, and in that moment of prayer she was set free. Sometimes we don't even know why we can't get close to God, can't get close to others, or can't even get along with ourselves. In most cases, the answer can be found in the mirror.

Next, spiritual intimacy requires Submission. The problem with submission is that it means we can't always have our way. It means that we aren't really in charge of as much as we think we are. Newsflash: We were never in charge. That's just another lie and distorted reality from the enemy to fool you and trick you into a false sense of security. True submission means, 'Not my will, but thy will be done, Lord.' It means, 'God I will release the grasp on what I think I want and submit to what you want for me.'

If you had asked me 20 years ago, here's what I wanted for my life: a high-paying corporate job in public relations; married with 2 or 3 beautiful children with good manners and no bad attitudes; a big house with a big yard; good friends; no problems. Sounds good, right? How did that turn out for me? Not quite—but oh, so much better.

I still remember a sermon that I heard when I was 10 years old. The preacher was talking about serving on the mission field for the Lord. He talked about evangelizing in isolated corners of the earth. He talked about harsh conditions that included unfriendly people, resistant attitudes to Christianity, famine and poverty-stricken areas that had little to no hope. My 10-year-old imagination constructed and envisioned a terrifying wasteland where no one would dare to venture. "Oh God, please don't ever ask me to do that," I whispered under my breath. After hearing that sermon, I quietly lived in fear that God would one day ask me to do whatever "mission work" was. More than 20 years later, God answered my prayer. His answer was, No. My request was denied, and I was headed overseas. Without hesitation or a conversation, God redirected my life toward mission work, despite my previous petition at age 10 for Him to exclude me from that calling.

In reality, nothing that I had feared about mission work was true. Indeed, it was simply my perception that was wrong. To be clear, all the things that I had heard and learned over the years were accurate, but they weren't necessarily true. I quickly realized that facts and truth are not always the same. Yes, there were harsh conditions. Yes, there was poverty. Yes, there was some resistance to new ideas and theology. But what never changed was God's promise or God's Word. Through every mile I traveled and every prayer I prayed, He was right there, ordering my steps and guiding my path. For every sick baby I held and every hopeless story I heard, His anointing was the light directing my steps. There was no fear in His presence, and there was no fear in His calling. Yes, there was sacrifice, but it also came with great reward.

Conclusion

In 2009, I walked down a dusty path in eastern Africa with a group of Ugandan children trailing on my heels. The air was dry, and the sun was beating down during its midday peak. I was sipping from a plastic bottle of water that had traveled thousands of miles with me from the United States. I was as curious about the children as they were about me. Although we looked similar to each other, I was a foreigner to them. When I stopped walking, they stopped walking. When I started walking, they started walking again too. When I turned around to address them, they stopped and stared; not directly at me, but at the precious bottle of water in my hand. They were accustomed to mission workers from afar, that was nothing new; their interest was in the bottle, which represented to them a valuable container to transport water. They desperately wanted my water bottle and followed me, awaiting the moment when I would discard it. From their past experiences, they knew the bottle meant nothing to me. Suddenly it became apparent to me, those children treasured my trash. Compared to them, it was clear that my life was easy, and I haven't had a bad day since then.

Submission to God's will for me has meant being called into ministry and called into missionary work in some very harsh places and conditions in some very poor environments. For decades, His will meant still being single into my 40s and not having any children of my own. His will has included a lot of long days, late nights, tears, and perceived disappointments. But it has also led to blessing countless people through ministry and spreading the Gospel to people all over this world.

Without question, my life has worked out better than I planned, because—for all intents and purposes—I'm in the perfect will of God for my life. Where else would I want to be? It worked out better because I understood that as I submitted to Christ, His will became my priority; meaning His will became my will. And guess what, when your will is in perfect alignment with the Father's will, the two become one.

You can have every single prayer answered when your will is in agreement with His. There will be no room for Disagreement, Discord, Disobedience, Diminishment, Displeasure, or Destruction. Because those things will be un-Desirable. Perfect agreement with God creates spiritual intimacy. I recognize that my life is solely for His glory—and yours is too.

Every day I thank God and give Him glory for His promises, His blessings, His peace, and the gift of victorious living that comes from the Anointing of Ease.

EASY LIFE ASSESSMENT

What un-Easy habits or activities below are you participating in that may be causing dis-Agreement or dis-Ease, and threatening your physical, spiritual, and emotional health and well-being? (Check all that apply)

☐ Junk food   ☐ Pornography
☐ Smoking   ☐ Infidelity/Lust
☐ Lack of exercise   ☐ Adultery/Fornication
☐ Drug use   ☐ Excessive spending
☐ Excessive alcohol   ☐ Dishonesty
☐ Gambling   ☐ Road rage/Anger
☐ Profanity   ☐ Procrastination
☐ Lack of focus   ☐ Jealousy/Envy

☐ Other

EASY LIVING

Do one of these a day, and in one month, your life will be easier:

- ☐ Say 'No' to one thing you honestly cannot do.
- ☐ Unsubscribe from one unimportant e-newsletter distribution or listserv.
- ☐ Apply the "one-touch" rule; open all your unopened mail and only touch it once to act, respond, file, or trash it.
- ☐ Delegate one task to someone else to lighten your load.
- ☐ Read Psalm 100 in the Bible aloud.
- ☐ Pay off one small bill or outstanding debt.
- ☐ Let go and release one pointless argument or disagreement.
- ☐ Give your keys a designated space in your home and put them there from now on.
- ☐ Demonstrate the love of Christ by performing a random act of kindness for someone you don't know.
- ☐ Select your wardrobe(s) the night before.
- ☐ Do something you enjoy—just for you.
- ☐ Read Psalm 23 in the Bible aloud.

- ☐ Ask for help on a project you planned to do alone.
- ☐ Sit quietly for 15 minutes before bedtime and just reflect and be thankful for all your blessings.
- ☐ Donate any clothes or shoes that you don't wear anymore to charity or to someone less fortunate.
- ☐ Read "The Anointing of Ease" in its entirety.
- ☐ Listen to one inspiring or motivational-minute podcast every day.
- ☐ Clear one cluttered surface in your home or office (table, desk, bed, etc.)
- ☐ Forgive and forget a small loan or debt that you know cannot be repaid.
- ☐ Read Matthew 11:28-30 in the Bible aloud.
- ☐ Tell someone you love that you love them.
- ☐ The next time someone offers to help, say yes and accept their assistance.
- ☐ Purchase an additional copy of "The Anointing of Ease" and bless someone else with it.
- ☐ Soak in a bubble bath.
- ☐ Place a monthly family To-Do list with tasks and deadlines on the refrigerator and celebrate together when the list is complete.
- ☐ Resist the urge to have the last word; choose instead to listen, learn, and love.

- ☐ Privately hide, block, un-friend, or un-follow a negative person or account on social media.
- ☐ Read Psalm 34 in the Bible aloud.
- ☐ Conduct an online search of this phrase: 'How many people live in poverty in the world?'—and be grateful for what you have.
- ☐ Complete this list and say a prayer of thanksgiving.

Thank you for purchasing this book. At least 10 percent of all proceeds from "The Anointing of Ease" book sales will be given as a tithe to continue and to support local ministries and international missionary work. God Bless you!

(Matthew 11:28-30, The Message Bible)
"Are you tired? Worn out? Burned out on religion? Come to me. Get away with me and you'll recover your life. I'll show you how to take a real rest. Walk with me and work with me—watch how I do it. Learn the unforced rhythms of grace. I won't lay anything heavy or ill-fitting on you. Keep company with me and you'll learn to live freely and lightly."

(Matthew 11:28-30, King James Version)
"Come unto me, all ye that labour and are heavy laden, and I will give you rest. Take my yoke upon you, and learn of me; for I am meek and lowly in heart: and ye shall find rest unto your souls. For my yoke is easy, and my burden is light."

Do you have a testimony or an encouraging story about God's anointing in your life that you would like to share? Visit www.AnointingOfEase.com for more information on how your testimony can be a blessing to others.

Contact Us

Website: www.AnointingOfEase.com

Email: Contact@AnointingOfEase.com

Facebook: Facebook.com/AnointingOfEase

Twitter: @AnointingOfEase
@vkfields

Write: Minister V.K. Fields
c/o Miracle Ministries Inc.
P.O. Box 18651
Raleigh, NC 27619

Notes:

Notes:

Notes:

----

www.ingramcontent.com/pod-product-compliance
Lightning Source LLC
Chambersburg PA
CBHW060352090426
42734CB00011B/2118